A History of Neath

From Earliest Times

A History of Neath

From Earliest Times

George Eaton

Christopher Davies Swansea

Published by
Christopher Davies (Publishers) Ltd.,
P.O. Box 403, Sketty,
Swansea, SA2 9BE.

ISBN 0 7154 0691 4

Printed in Wales

Bound by
Geo Tremewan & Son Ltd.,
Neath.

CONTENTS

FOREWORD

The publication of 'From Castle to Civic Centre' in January 1974 evoked considerable interest and it led to requests for a reprint. Publishers Christopher Davies Ltd., of Swansea intimated that they would be interested in publishing a new and enlarged edition of the above work. I considered, and they agreed, that perhaps it would meet more fully the needs of readers if a comprehensive history of Neath from prehistoric times to the present day was produced, incorporating 'From Castle to Civic Centre'. Such then is the scope of this book.

ACKNOWLEDGEMENTS

I would like to record my acknowledgements to the staff of the following Libraries and Museums for the considerable help and cooperation received from them:

The National Library of Wales, the Library of Swansea University; the Central Library at Swansea and Neath (West Glamorgan), the National Museum of Wales, the County Record Office and its branch in West Glamorgan. I would also wish to record my thanks to the officers and staff of the Neath Borough Council. Finally, I would like to thank my wife for many valuable suggestions.

GEORGE EATON

CHAPTER 1

Pre-history

The Paleolithic Era

Tracing our racial origins is fraught with much difficulty because for very long periods no evidence has appeared of any human habitation. But although there existed these long gaps, there is general agreement that there is a time scale of over 250,000 years covering the existence of Homo Sapiens. In 1953 a primitive stone axehead was picked up on an allotment in Penylan Cardiff belonging to the Achelian age some 200,000 years ago. In Paviland Cave, Rhossili, a Miss Cunningham discovered a flake tool left behind by Homo Sapiens Neanderthalemis 70,000 years ago. This was composed of siliceous sandstone, a common substitute for flint in the west. It belonged to Mousterian culture of the Middle Paleolithic period. Man of this type were slow footed with a slouching gait.

During the long periods of time there had been many fluctuations in climatic conditions and, during interglacial periods, small groups of man appeared intermittently. Following the Mousterian age, a long glacial phase followed during which habitation was denied man. Then almost 30,000 years ago, a warmer phase emerged which allowed renewed human habitation. Men of a modern type came from Central Europe. These were designated Homo Sapiens Sapiens (true man). Fortunately a skeleton of such a type was found in Paviland Cave in 1823, which was to prove the richest site of archeological finds in the whole of Britain. Evidence of habitation were found in Nottle Tor, Long Hole and Cathole in Gower. But the only human remains were discovered in Paviland which proved to be the richest of Aurignacian sites.

Following a visit by amateur archeologists, Miss Talbot of Penrice and W. Dilwyn, the Swansea pottery manufacturer, to Paviland, a quantity of the teeth of cave bears were found. This brought Dr Buckland, Professor of Geology at Oxford (the first post of its kind) to the scene. He made the exciting discovery of a headless skeleton stained with red ochre and closely associated with ivory rods and rings and quantities of sea shells. This skeleton became known as the 'Red Lady of Paviland' until Professor

Reconstruction of the burial of the 'Red Lady' of Paviland.
(By permission of the National Museum of Wales).

Sollas in 1912 discovered it was that of a young male of 25 years old. A ritual burial was suggested with the staining with red ochre suggesting a life-giving colour of blood. Dr Buckland, a Christian Minister (later to be Dean of Westminster), could hardly admit the skeleton to be older than that from the antideluvian age.

It would be difficult to find a more excellent site for human habitation. The cave is a narrow cleft in a limestone cliff overlooking the Bristol Channel which was then a broad wooded valley teeming with wild life.

The skeleton was placed in the University Museum at Oxford. There M. Cartellon identified it as belonging to the Aurignacian period of the Upper Paleolithic Age and in 1912, Professor Sollas and the French anthropologist Abbé Breuil confirmed this, and also described it as a young male of 25 years old belonging to the Cromagnon race (named after a site in Southern France where other human remains were found). These were tall strong people with prominent chins and high-bridged noses. Their brain capacity was high. They were as close to our conception of the 'noble savage' as could be. Their tools showed an amazing range of techniques adopted for various specialised uses. They probably possessed a primitive religion suggested by the ritual burying. Long periods living in close proximity in caves would have probably encouraged a form of language. There was really very little difference in appearance to modern man. Jacquetta Hawkes, the anthropologist, in fact described the Cro-Magnon man as 'our brother'!

Professor Sollas and Abbé Breuil found no less than 3,400 flake instruments of various kinds in the cave of Middle and Upper Aurignacian Age; bones of the woolly rhinoceros, mammoth, hyena and cave bear with a wide range of stone and bone implements. Carbon dating has established the age of the skeleton as 16,500 years old with another bone as 20,000 years old. Revised dating suggests 18,000 years as age for the skeleton. The exciting technique of carbondating (the measuring of radio-active isotopes from organic material) was discovered by Professor Libby of Chicago University in 1950 as a by-product of nuclear physics research. This has become increasingly sophisticated in recent years as seen in the work of Dr McBurney in his examination of prehistoric remains in such Gower Caves such as Cathole and that of Professor Green in his analysis of remains in Pontnewydd, the Vale of Clwyd. A further examination of the Paviland skeleton is planned.

Paviland Cave. Early Upper Palaeolithic finds; left to right: (a) leaf point, (b) burin busqué, (c) keeled scraper, (d) end of blade scraper, (e) tang of Font Robert point. *(By permission of the National Museum of Wales).*

There have been no signs of the dazzling cave paintings of the French and Spanish caves. It was thought at one time that some red marks in Bacon Hole were signs of some artistic activity of prehistoric man, but now it is generally accepted that they are of natural origin. The renewal of glaciation after 16,000 B.C. drove Cro-Magnon man southwards and he did not appear until 13,000 B.C. It is thought by some anthropologists that this culture did not come directly from France which may explain the absence of the extraordinary artistic feats found in the caves of Altimira, Lascaux, Font de Guare and Niax.

Mesolithic Age

After the end of the last glaciation c. 8,000 B.C. conditions emerged into a steppe-like flora and fauna world where the wild ox and pig found plentiful grazing land. The cave period had now come to an end and with it came a mild, damp, climate favourable to the growth of trees. The sub-divisions of the stone age have only a chronological significance. There was no clear line of transition, only a gradual merging and overlapping. Improvements in weapon techniques took place with bone and wooden shafts fitted on the older cave implements. Great numbers of microlithes (arrow and harpoon heads) were found. (Amateur archeologists such as Mr S. Price of Treherbert, collected large numbers of microlithes in the Craig-y-Llyn district). The end of the Wurm glaciation had melted ice fields and the released water drove man inland and away from his previous hunting grounds. Plant and animal life spread over areas of higher land and deer and great horned cattle (a skeleton of one was recently found) became common and fish were plentiful. It is possible that some of the blood of mesolithic people still flows in our veins but such ethnic elements must be very small.

Neolithic Age

This used to be called the New Stone Age or the age of Polished Stone. It is now more generally described as the age of Farmers. The coming of the Neolithic people signalled a complete revolution in the economy with the return of a warm dry climate at about 2000 B.C. The belt of marshy land along the coast below Neath and Swansea had encouraged settlement inland and stock raising, hunting and more important crop cultivation now took place. With crop cultivation came a settled life style. These people were dark haired and stocky. They were called Iberians (the 'shy trafficers' in Matthew Arnold's poem). They came from Mediterranean lands reaching Britain by way of Spain and France. Quite probably some came via Ireland as similarities between Irish monuments in New Grange and those in Anglesey can plainly be discerned. They came to Wales and Ireland probably as prospectors of tin and copper and exported some back to Mediterranean lands.

Polished stone axes have been found in Aberdulais and Melincryddan testifying to their presence in this district. The axehead found in an allotment in a garden at Cefn-yr-allt was a product of the famous axe factory at Craig Llwyd, North Wales, suggesting extensive mobility in that age. Another implement was found in the Melin Tinplate Works but this was unfortunately lost.

Among the stone remains left by these Neolithic people are standing stones, very prevalent in Gower but represented in Neath by one in Cwrt School playground. An even larger one was found on Drymmau (Carn Bica). What is the significance of these? We do not know for certain but the usual suggestion is that they are memorial stones. Some writers see some significance in the Biblical story of Jacob, the Patriarch, whose wife Rachel died over 3,000 years ago 'And Jacob set up a pillar of stone upon her grave, that is the pillar of Rachel's grave to this day'. A recent suggestion is that they were signalling stones marking ancient routes.

The Neolithic people are specially associated with the building of large impressive chambered tombs. A typical example is Tinkinswood, near St Nicholas and several occur in Gower. Briton Ferry is probably the site of one of these massive Cromlechs; now destroyed but perpetuated by the name Giants Grave. The most remarkable fact in the early history of Wales was the moving of a number of stones from the Presely Mountains in Pembrokeshire to the Wiltshire Downs in the building of Stonehenge. A miracle of transportation. It seems that they were responsible for the first building of Stonehenge and Avebury which the later Bronze Age folk completed. It is to the Bronze Age people that we most attribute the stone circles and cairns on March Hywel, Cefn Ffordd and Drymmau.

Bronze Age

Between 2000 and 1500 B.C. came the Beaker People, so-called because of their practice of planting in their graves small brown drinking cups (beakers). Their graves were single tombs under round mounds contrasting with the Neolithic chambered tombs. It is a peculiar fact that these stone builders did not build homes that have survived (apart from those at Stormy Down and St Davids). Glyn Daniels points out that Wales looked two ways; eastwards to England and westwards to Ireland. This dichotomy of outlook is one of the priceless and invigorating features of our early Welsh heritage.

The beaker folk were early metallurgists making copper and gold

Bronze axehead found at Bryncoch. *(By permission of the National Museum of Wales).*

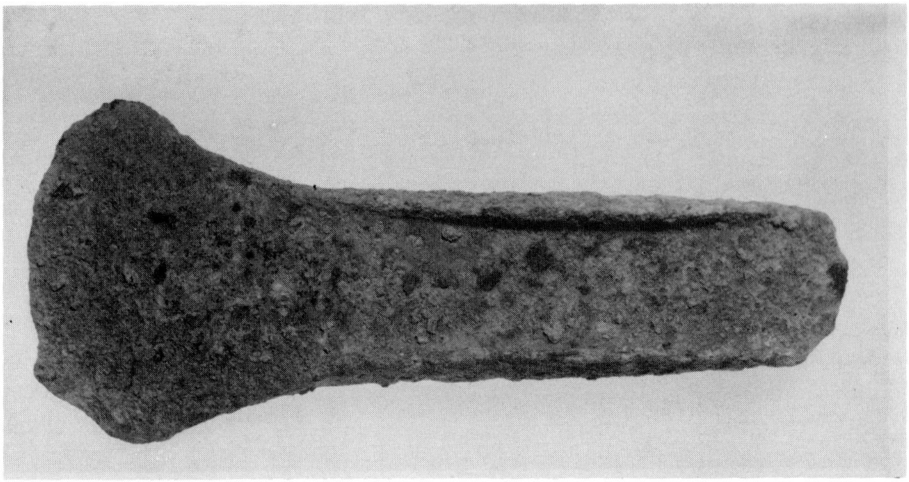

Bronze tankard handles of early Iron Age type, from the Seven Sisters hoard, Cadoxton-juxta-Neath. *(By permission of the National Museum of Wales).*

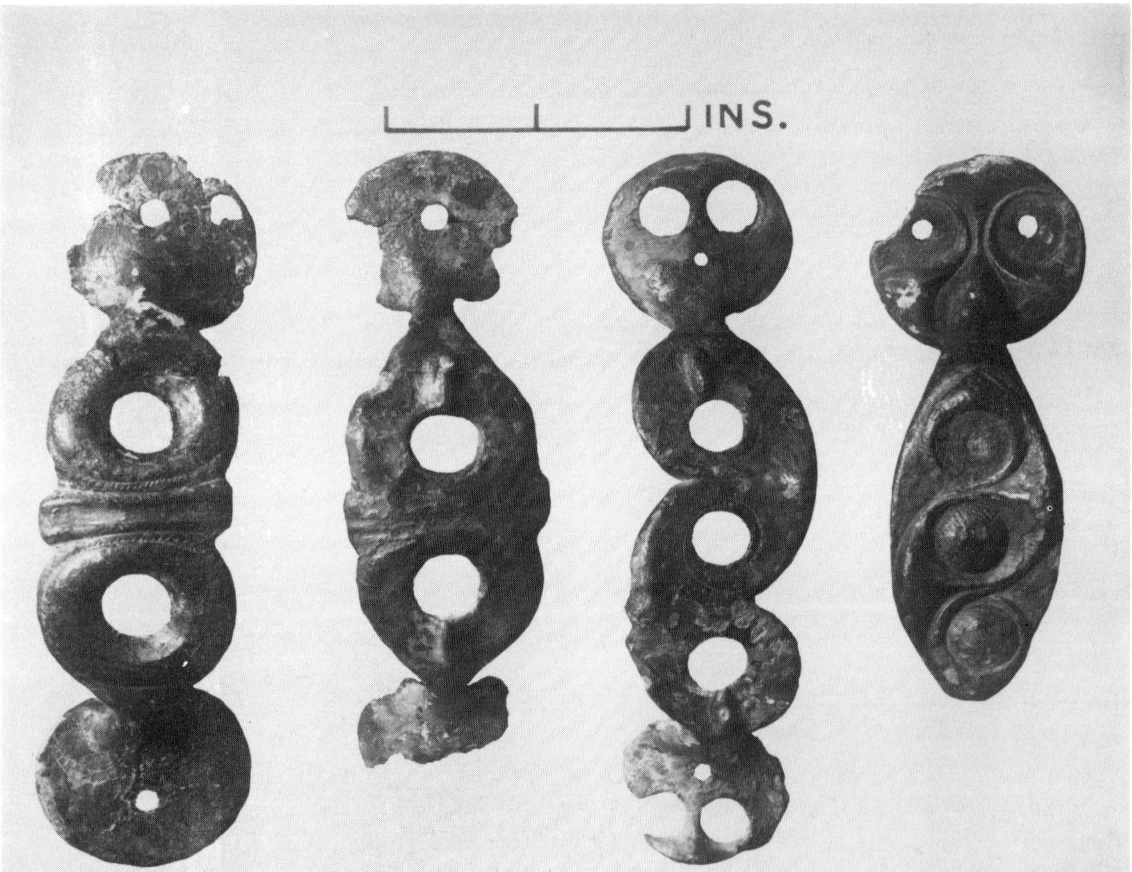

objects. There were no beakers found in Neath although a coarse specimen was found in Llanmadoc in Gower. These beakers were assumed to have some ritual purpose and were often referred to as incense cups. More sophisticated cups were found in Llantristant and Merthyr Mawr. The small earthen pot found in the upper Nedd area, perpetuated by the farm name of Carn-y-Crockan, may have belonged to the beaker folk.

Later Bronze Age people left a flanged bronze axehead in a Bryncoch garden which was found by Mr O. Griffiths and deposited by him in the National Museum. This was a rare find in Wales. On Crymlyn Burrows was discovered an unlooped bronze axe (c. 1400 B.C.) now preserved in the Royal Institution in Swansea. Belonging to a later age, (c. 900-1200 B.C.) was a bronze socket loop found above the Scwd Einon Gam Waterfall now in the National Museum. The people who used these implements trickled in from Southern England where they built the later phases of Stonehenge and Avebury. A compartively quiet period came to an end about 1000 B.C. This was the late Bronze Age.

Then there was unrest caused by social and economic disturbances which followed the first exploitation of iron.

The Iron Age and the Cult of the Celts

From the third to the seventh century B.C. Celtic Tribes were moving across Europe in many directions showing a vigour in migration equal to any who came after them. The word "Celt" comes from the Greek 'Keltoi' or the Latin 'Celtae' which were the words of ancient Greeks used for the so-called Barbarian nations of Central Europe. The Celtic invaders of Britain came in successive waves with dialects of their own. Erse, Gaelic and Welsh are still extant variations of the Celtic tongue. The Iberian peoples were driven westwards into Cornwall, Wales, Ireland and northwards into Scotland by the newcomers. They were tall and fair unlike the dark Iberians. One of the Celtic groups, the Brythonic people, occupied Wales. The iron weapons used by Celtic tribes were irresistible and a Celtic aristocracy was established over the native Iberians.

Llyn Fawr Hoard

In the transition from the Bronze to the Iron Age there appeared not so much single discoveries as hoards which were collections of objects belonging to what appeared to be some kind of travelling salesmen.

The Llyn Fawr Hoard was a collection of bronze and iron implements discovered when the lake was converted into a reservoir in 1911. It ranks as one of the most important finds in Wales. It included, amongst other things, two splendid cauldrons of Hiberno-British type, socketed axe-

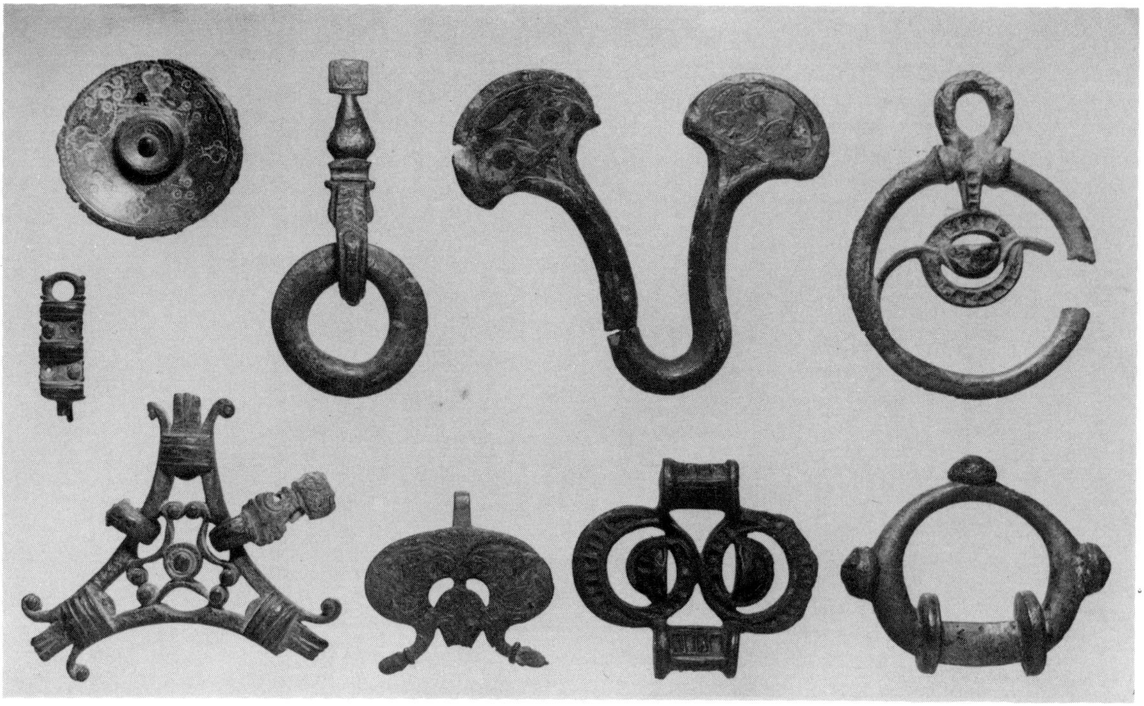

A part of hoard containing horse harnesses of early Iron Age and Roman types, from Seven Sisters, Cadoxton-juxta-Neath.
(By permission of the National Museum of Wales).

heads, bronze harness fittings of contemporary continental origin and a razor. There was also found a part of an iron sword, the only Hallstadt type found in Britain. We have no certain knowledge of how or why they were deposited but it is probable that a party of exploring Celts must have reached this wild spot and recognized in this gloomy remote lake a fitting abode for their gods whom they would like to propitiate. To the Celts Gods were everywhere about them but water in springs, lakes and rivers were especially holy. So they took what they could probably ill spare, the implements described above, and deposited them in a slow, sacrificial submergence in the dark lake. Professor Grimes sees an Irish origin in many of these objects.

Iron Age Hill Forts

The principal field artiquities of the Celts were not burial places, as in previous cultures, but fortified settlements. Tribal hostilities led them to build hill forts or sometimes fortified farm houses. A damper and colder climate in the first millenium resulted in most of these settlements being established on small hills near the coast. In the Neath area, the hill forts are of smaller types compared to the Cil-Ivor Fort in Gower and Mynydd-y-Castell in Margam. Among the larger types in the Neath district is Buachy-Gaer, a hill fort on Mynydd-y-Gaer, a hill overlooking Margam with a more elaborate earthwork lower down called Y Gaer Fawr. Another Iron Age enclosure with marked defensive features lies on a spur on the south side of the hill. Warren Hill is a site of another fort. This is a strong bivallate type which probably had an important function relating to the mouth of the River Neath. No excavations have been made of these forts.

A number of hitherto unrecorded enclosures have been recorded by Mr L. P. Cockwell. The first is a roughly circular earthwork with signs of ditching. To the north/north east is an earthwork that again is roughly circular which slopes away on all sides. A walk known locally as 'Ladies Walk' skirts the eastern side. These hill forts, like others in Wales, probably belong to the second stage of the Iron Age culture called La Tene (from La Tene in Switzerland). There is little evidence of the third stage in Wales. Certainly none in Neath. This stage refers to the Belgae, a people of mixed Celtic and Teutonic stock. However, a great deal of excavation work needs to be done on these hill forts before we get a real picture of the life style of the Celts.

We know they had a distinctive language which we term 'British'. This much can be deducted from the statements of Greek travellers but the absence of Celtic writings make our knowledge very slight. Many relics of the Iron Age have been found in other parts of Wales. Nearest to Neath are Iron Age sites in Merthyr Mawr where pottery and metal objects have been found. Elsewhere there have been discovered intricate brooches of bronze,

Celtic coin with chariot scene.

gold and iron work tankards, harness fittings, bowls, all exquisitely ornamental.

Further up the Neath Valley, Iron Age settlements were discovered by Harry Green on the hillside overlooking Merlin Court Brook. Some of these were simply fortified farm houses. Generally associated with the Iron Age, some of these were probably pre-Celtic and some even British.

Apart from stockraising, crops of barley and wheat were sown. Barley was grown widely and was much used for brewing beer, the national drink of the Celts. Everywhere Julius Caesar was told that the Celts knew nothing of agriculture and lived on meat and milk and dressed in skins. As in many things, he was badly informed. Even in remote areas before the Romans came the soil was cultivated and people dressed in woollen and linen clothes.

The Celts were a highly imaginative and superstitious race and were dominated by the Druids, a priesthood occupying a special place in the higher echelons of Celtic society. This esoteric sect was very learned in religion, law and medicine and acted as intermediaries between the tribe and the many gods the Celts believed in. Their power over the people was greatly feared by the Romans who sought, successfully, to destroy them. Having no written language, the Druids committed everything to memory but this oral translation was expressed in writing in the 7th and 8th centuries writings. The bardic tradition continued into the Middle Ages when it flourished splendidly.

Amongst the Celts the head was venerated above all else for they believed the head was the repository of the soul and of life itself, a symbol of divinity and power over the gods of the other world. This led to the cult of the severed head which tended to dominate their art. Their mysticism also led them to believe in a form of reincarnation.

The genius of the Celts was seen in their brilliant art of decorative metal work and also in such practical things as their mastery of the spoked wheel, especially the ingenuity of being able to attach iron rims on to wooden wheels. This enabled them to be masters of chariot warfare. It is not surprising to find them venerating the horse. The White Horse of Uffingham is a brilliant artistic expression of the essential spirit of the horse.

CHAPTER 2

The Romans in Wales

Unlike the Celts, who were illiterate, the Romans were comparatively highly sophisticated. Their written records were extensive. The Antonine Itinerary of the third century had long made known the existence of the Fort Nidum. It was not, however, until 1949 that the exact location was revealed. During the construction of a housing estate in Roman Way, the late Stanley Thomas was shown pieces of samian ware that were dug up. These were identified by Dr Nash Williams of the National Museum as features of a Roman Fort. Nidum had at last been found. Subsequent excavations by Dr Swinburne in 1858 confirmed this and established the fact that the original fort was a timber one which had been burnt down c. 75-80 A.D. A second timber fort was build after an interval of abandonment. A stone fort was then built during 120 and 125 A.D. with rampart walls and gateways, the remains of two gateways still remaining. The fort played an important part in the Roman Conquest especially under Julius Frontinus.

Later strategy by the Romans was more concerned with establishing a frontier zone in the Vale of Neath between the Silures and the Demetae tribes to prevent any united action by them. Many of the Roman marching camps were established between Tonna and the Roman Camp at Gwelbren. The one in Tonna (situated at Blaencwmbach) is the largest known in Wales. A Roman force on campaign would need 20 acres (c. 8 hectares) per 5000 men. This 62 acre site could, therefore, provide for 15,000. Professor Jarret refers to this as an overwhelming force but he considered the site a temporary one.

The auxiliary fort at Coelbren, probably built at the same time as Nidum, was also in the nature of a marching camp. The main causeway from Neath to Coelbren and thence to Y Gaer at Brecon is Sarn Helen, a ridge road running along the crest of Hirfynydd avoiding the forests and swamps of the lower ground. Along this road, and still discernible for long stretches, are a number of small square enclosures (unexcavated) which are almost certainly Roman signal stations. It seemed that the Roman

Roman coin with
chariot scene.

Excavation of
Nidum.
*(By permission of the
National Museum of
Wales).*

strategy was to pierce the uplands with attacks on the Neath and Usk Valleys. (Incidentally, Sir Cyril Fox has demonstrated that Sarn Helen was still used in the Middle Ages by horsemen and pack horses).

But Nidum itself must have had some function despite this strategy for it was mentioned in the Antonine Itinerary. Dr Savory suggests that it might have served as a staging post in the imperial courier service after its disuse as a fort. But the coast, for a long time was an important line of communication as the Milestones found along the road testify. One which was dedicated to the Emperor Diocletian was found by Mr Brooks Taylor whilst excavating for clay in the Millands. This is now preserved in the National Museum. Halfway between Briton Ferry and Baglan was found another milestone dedicated to Victorinus, a Roman Governor in Gaul and later in Britain.

There is no doubt that the Romans met fierce resistance from the Silures despite the enormous superiority of the Romans in numbers. It is a common assumption that the Silures were Celts but Tacitus, the Roman historian, describes them as having black, curly hair and of stocky build. These were quite different in appearance from the Celtic tribes that the Romans had encountered in England, Iberian stock probably.

Reconstruction of Maen Stone, near Ystradfellte. *(By permission of the National Museum of Wales).*

Recent excavations in Roman Way revealed part of the road that linked the Roman Fort Nidum with that of the fort at Loughor.
(By permission of Mr Lightfoot).

It is doubtful whether there were many Romans from Italy in the occupation. Tribes from several countries in Europe were now fighting under the Roman Flag as part of the wider Roman Empire. What of the native population during the three-hundred odd years of Roman occupation? Modern evidence suggests that they returned to their hill forts and men built new ones with the permission of their Roman masters. They lived much in their old ways but certainly accepted many of the portable benefits of Roman civilisation such as fine pottery dishes, glass bottles, bronze saucepans, mirrors and brooches. Roman dress was often copied and Latin strongly influenced the national language.

Towards the end of the 4th century unrest and discord was spreading in the Empire. Britain became drained of fighting men and became open to barbarian attacks. In 383 A.D. a Spanish-born commander, Magnus Maximus, established himself as ruler of Britain and France. He figures in Welsh legend as Macsin Wledig, a king of Rome who was impelled by a marvellous dream to journey across the mountains and sea to a fort in Arfon where he would meet his future wife, Helen. Somehow this legend captured the imagination of the early Welsh and the name Helen has been perpetuated in many stretches of roads (e.g. Sarn Helen). Macsin Wledig is a shadowy figure in our history but very prominent in folklore.

Recent Excavations at Nidum

The Glamorgan and Gwent Archeological Trust have been carrying out excavations at Nidum and many artefacts have been unearthed. Many ceramic finds have been made including samian, mortarian and amphora ware with a complete jar of grey ware. A number of floor tiles have also been found. Part of a road that probably led from Neath to Loughor has been discovered.

The National Museum and the Ministry also have been involved in this project.

Milestone dedicated to Emperor Diocletian.
(By permission of the NLW).

CHAPTER 3

The Age of Saints

The legacy of the Romans consisted of Christianity, a road system and a permanent linguistic heritage of borrowed words from the Latin. But there was certainly no latinisation as there was in Gaul. Christianity was a strong foreign cult followed by a few Roman soldiers and officials and much less popular than the cult of Mithras; and certainly less than the native celtic deities. The remains of a small Christian Church in Caerwent is the only known one.

The Celtic Church seems to have arisen from the fusion of Gaulo-Roman Christianity of Roman occupation days. Between the fifth and eighth centuries A.D. the whole country was christianised by wandering monks and missionaries of the Celtic Church. These were later called Saints although they were not officially canonised by the Catholic Church. Many of these came from Gaul and in this way Christianity was spread after the Romans departed. Some of these Saints set up cells which afterwards became Churches bearing their name. Some churches bear the name of these saints but have no direct relationship. In Neath we have St Cadoc and St Illtud but there is no real evidence of any precise relationship with these saints. The word 'llan' originally meant 'enclosure' but it became associated with a church because it was the custom for any of these early saints to fence off a piece of ground around their cells.

The history of the centuries which followed the departure of the Romans is very sketchy and comprised of a few memorial pillar stones (Hence the term 'Dark Ages'). A fragment of a sixth century stone now in the Royal Institution, Swansea is the one of the surviving monuments of the immediate post-Roman period. This stone was taken from Sarn Helen at a spot near Coelbren and placed in the Gnoll Grotto in a collection of stones made by Lady Mackworth (widow of Sir Robert Mackworth). The inscription is debased but it could read that Macaritinus, son of Bericus, lies near this stone. Near Ystradfellte, on the Sarn Helen causeway, is a better preserved stone, Maen Madoc, 11 feet high. On the black moorland

Gnoll Grotto,
Macaration Stone.
(By permission of the National Museum of Wales).

was buried one Derbag, son of Justus. A more famous one is the Bodvac Stone found on Margam Mountain and now housed in Margam Stone Museum. The stones demonstrate the Roman tradition of roadside burials which survived until the 6th century or even later. The inscriptions are a mingling of Roman and Celtic names in the Romano-British tradition.

Of a later century is a sculptured stone fragment which was found in Coelbren and deposited in the Gnoll Grotto collection together with the Macaritin stone. These were deposited in the Royal Institution in 1923. It is fervently hoped that they will be allowed to return to Neath where there is now a Borough Museum. The sculptured fragment, a very valuable relic, contains a disc-headed slab-cross of a style characteristic of West Glamorgan in the 9th and 10th centuries. Near the top is part of a wheeled cross whilst below is part of a male figure wearing a kind of kilt or apron with hands raised in prayer. A tall pillar-stone with an incised Latin cross occur in Cwrt Herbert and a cross-incised pillar at Melin-Cwrt with slab crosses at Baglan, Llantwit, Bryn Ceithin, and Cwm Gwernffrawd which are of 9th century origin. Here the Roman tradition of roadside burials are combined with the earlier practice of recording the ancestry of the deceased. Those commemorated were doubtless members of the ruling class. However we know very little indeed about those post-Roman centuries; merely echoes from these sparse memorial stones and a great deal of imagination.

The Foundations of the Welsh Language and Culture

The history of the Welsh language involved an evolution by which its basic nature changed completely during the sixth century. This linguistic change was a rapid one from an older language which we call British. We know little about this language because there are no written records. However from classical authors, Roman official documents and Latin inscriptions, we can glean some idea of its nature. The British language was in fact not dissimilar to the Latin of the Romans for it had case endings which did the work of prepositions just as is Latin. Many British and Latin words were made up of two words with a linking vowel and there was also a similarity in pronunciation. All this made it easy for the British to borrow Latin words during the Romano-British period. The rate of linguistic change intensified after the Roman occupation and by the 6th century a new language was born. Dr Jackson who has expertly analysed this matter asks the question, 'How old is the Weldh language?' and he supplies the answer that Welsh is as old as the sixth century.

French is a language that arose in a similar way. From a colloquial Latin spoken by the French during the Roman occupation, by the 9th century, the French language appeared without case endings. Another change appeared in primitive Welsh. This is called soft mutation affecting the consonant between two vowels producing the word Caradoc from the Latin Caractacus. Anglicisation of Welsh words have produced Malvern from Maelfryn and Dover from Dwfr. A more complicated word change took place when Sabrina (British for the present Severn) became Hafren in Welsh and to the English Hafren became Hevern or Severn. During the 8th century Welsh became a written language called Old Welsh which was not very different from modern Welsh.

Ancient tales orally handed down became the subject matter for the poets in the early Middle Ages. The first poet recorded is Talhaearn (c.550). Later the names of Aneirin and Taliesin appear but it was not until the 13th century that the works of these two people are recorded in full versions. The best known prophetic poem was "Armes Prydern" (c.990) and was probably written by a monk. The later Middle Ages produced the great literature of the four branches of the Mabinogion and Arthurian legends.

CHAPTER 4

The Establishment of the Borough

Before the 12th century was many years old a castellated borough ("burgus") was established by a Norman Knight, Richard de Granville, on the banks of the River Nedd, near the present ruins of Neath Abbey. It commanded coastal and valley routes, access to the sea and a river crossing. Outside the settlement were forests and swamps and, up in the hills, were the scattered homesteads of bitterly resentful native Welsh, including those who had been dispossessed by the invaders but who had managed to escape. As a defensive measure against inevitable guerilla attacks, a castle, almost certainly of the primitive motte and bailey type, was thrown up aided probably, by the forced labour of Welsh prisoners. This type of castle, built by the Normans during their initial settlements, was little more than a slender fortress of stakes and turf consisting of a mound ("motte") on which the lord's dwelling was build and protected by a palisade of stakes. A surrounding courtyard (the "bailey") housed the lord's men and horses which, in turn, was protected by a palisade and ditch.

The settlement was part of a territory embracing a large area between the Nedd and the Afan over which de Granville claimed a very superficial overlordship. It was at the western extremity of the lordship of Glamorgan and Morgannwg, the greatest of all the Marcher Lordships created by the Norman Lords. This was a region wrested by the latter from the last ruler of Morgannwg, Iestyn ap Gwrgant.

Under the Welsh Princes, it was divided into three hundreds (cantrefi). These hundreds were divided, in turn, into commotes (cwmwdau) which existed as almost self-sufficient units, under the overlordship of one prince or king. The commotes were further divided into trefi which were small straggling communities, unlike the more compact English villages. These ancient tribal divisions were taken over by the Normans and turned into their own feudal estates.

To record the manner of the conquest of Morgannwg creates, however, immediate difficulties, because of the lack of documentary evidence. The popular story of the conquest has been narrated by 16th century writers such as Sir Edward Stradling of St Donats, Rhys Meurig of Cottrell and David Powell of Ruabon, the latter publishing Stradling's version in his "Historie of Cambria" in 1584. One copy of Stradling's work, concerning the history of his own pedigree and of the conquest of Glamorgan by Robert Fitzhamon and his twelve knights, had come into the possession of a remarkable Welsh lady at the court of Elizabeth. This was Mrs Blanche Parry, a relative of Sir Edward. She was Queen Elizabeth's personal maid, keeper of the Queen's jewellery and enjoyed much influence as the Court Astrologer. One of her friends was David Powell to whom she gave her copy of Stradling's book. It was this action that set in train a story that was to dominate historical writing about the Norman conquest for centuries to come. It remained accepted history almost up to modern times but now it is merely part of legendary history, although the tenacity of this story of the "Twelve Knights" has influenced the naming of a popular hotel.

The tale itself is too well known to narrate in detail. Besides, there are many versions. The main facts concern a quarrel between Iestyn ap Gwrgant of Morgannwg and Rhys ap Tewdwr, the powerful Prince of Deheubarth in the latter years of the 11th century. It arose from the jealousy of Iestyn when he heard of how Rhys had become fascinated by his (Iestyn) wife, whose beauty had been lavishly praised by the bards. Following a quarrel during a meeting at Neath between the two Princes, an attack on Morgannwg was planned by Rhys.

Iestyn sent one of his supporters, Einion ap Collwyn to the court of King Rufus to seek his support against Rhys ap Tewdwr. This materialised under the leadership of Rupert Fitzhamon and, in the ensuing battle at Hirwaun, Rhys was killed. The Normans were paid in gold on the Golden Mile near Bridgend (this was largely a story to fit place names!) Einion, however, did not receive the hand in marriage of Iestyn's daughter as his promised reward and, incensed at this betrayal, persuaded the Normans to return. Iestyn was defeated and driven from his lands. This, we are told, was how Fitzhamon and his twelve knights settled in the Vale of Glamorgan (Bro Morgannwg) leaving the hill districts (Blaenau Morgannwg) to the descendants of Iestyn.

The Golden Lion on a Blue Shield. Attributed to Robert Fitzhamon, although the early Normans did not have personal armorial shields.

It is an ancient tale, deeply entrenched in bardic tradition, but unacceptable as authentic history. Rhys ap Tewdwr was, of course, killed in Brecon in 1093, whilst attempting to stem an invasion by the Norman, Bernard Newmarch. Yet the story could contain an element of distorted fact like so many legends. Bitter rivalries certainly existed between Welsh chieftains and a precedent existed for bringing in Norman aid when Caradoc ap Gruffydd (Iestyn's predecessor in Morgannwg) enlisted Norman support against Mareddud ap Owen in 1071. It is not improbable that the ambitious Rhys sought to establish a firm overlordship over Morgannwg.

When Sir Edward Stradling's account of the conquest of Glamorgan is considered, inaccuracies and perhaps, even deliberate fabrications emerge. Stradling named twelve knights who had been assigned lordships in the Marcher lordship created by Fitzhamon. Professor Ralph Griffiths has provided a valuable analysis of when their names first appeared in Glamorgan history. Only four of the twelve appear to have genuine claims to be the original followers of Fitzhamon, namely William de Londres, Gilbert de Umframville of Penarth, Robert le Sor of Peterson and St Quentin of Talyfan.

Richard de Granville is not included amongst these knights but a strong claim could reasonably be made for the founder of Neath Borough for, in his gift of lands for the founding of Neath Abbey, Monknash was included which was later to become one of the Abbey's largest granges. This was land in the Vale which was occupied during Fitzhamon's time. As for the remaining names, they appear at various times during the succeeding two centuries from the Turbervilles, who appeared early enough to be a signatory to de Granville's foundation charter to the monks at Neath Abbey, to the Stradlings who did not arrive at St Donats until the end of the 13th century. The family was not, in fact, Norman at all. The first Stradling came from Strattlingen (Switzerland) in the reign of Edward 1, but was never in the possession of a Welsh estate. The connection between the Stradlings and St Donats came about by the marriage of Peter, Sir Edward's son, to Joan de Hawey, the heiress of St Donats. In other words, the first seven generations of Stradlings at St Donats were pure legends.

Sir Edward Stradling was a man of wide culture, the ideal of a Renaissance gentleman, friend of Raleigh, Gilbert, Drake and Burleigh. He was particularly attached to antiquarian studies and was very anxious, indeed determined, to prove his pedigree back to the original conquerors of Glamorgan even to sacrificing historical truth in the process. It was a very marked characteristic of the Welsh in Tudor times to regard pedigree as the hall-mark of social standing. Many of the gentry relied upon Stradling to provide them with ancient pedigrees. Lord Burleigh, the great Elizabethan statesman, was one such person. One Brecon squire claimed descent from King Arthur of the Round Table! This produced some scoffing lines from one Englishman writing:

"Pye Gott they be all Shentlemen
Was descended from Shove none lyne (Jove's own line)
Parte humane parte divine . . .
And Venus, that fayre Goddesse,

And twenty other shentleboddies (bodies)
Hector Stoute and Comely Paris
Arthur Prutus, King of Ffayres."

It is, of course, a great misfortune that the probable source of much of what appeared relating to the history of Glamorgan, is lost. This was the "Register of Neath" which was referred to by Rhys Meurig in a manuscript copy of his book. It has now disappeared but a chronicle by the monks of Margam (Annales de Margam) has survived and contains many references to Glamorgan. The monks of Neath and Margam were, undoubtedly, keenly interested in history. Travelling bands, who flourished greatly in Medieval times, were warmly welcomed at the abbeys and spread the stories they had heard far and wide.

How, then, was the conquest effected? By 1070, it is certain that a prominent Norman knight, William Fitzosborn, had been granted the Earldom of Hereford by King William. Large territories were annexed by Fitzosborn, castles built, and the greater part of the Welsh population were allowed to retain their ancient customs. Inroads were made into Gwent and strongholds erected at Chepstow and Caerleon. He then left for Flanders, where he was killed in 1071. The King, apparently, did not encourage any further conquests in South Wales by his followers, probably because of the rebellious behaviour of Fitzosborn's son.

In 1081, we find him making a visit to St Davids, probably with the double objective of carrying out a pilgrimage and of making a treaty with Rhys ap Tewdwr to pacify the Welsh. However, the King's death in 1087 changed the climate and a meeting arranged with the new King Rufus and Robert Fitzhamon in Gloucester, in 1089, may have been the occasion of plans being made for a renewed campaign of conquest. Fitzhamon, lord of Cruelly, in Normandy, had show consistent loyalty to both William and Rufus (it was he who tried to dissuade the latter from his fateful hunt in the New Forest by reporting to the King a monk's dream of forboding). He was rewarded with extensive lands in Gloucester and his marriage to Sybil, daughter of the powerful, Roger, Earl of Shrewsbury, enhanced his growing status.

Nothing is known of the details of the actual conquest of Glamorgan. Some historians argue in favour of a seaborne invasion from Bristol, others that it was from already established in Gwent. What is evident is that by 1105, when Fitzhamon left for service in Normandy, he had established an overlordship from Usk to the Tawe. As for the pattern of conquest, we can only assume that a troop of mailed knights, with men at arms mounted and on foot, fought their way westwards acrss the lowlands plains of Glamorgan (following almost certainly the old Roman road) dispossessing the small scattered communities of the native Welsh and establishing, at various strategic points, hastily constructed motte and bailey wooden castles to ward off the inevitable counter-attacks from the native Welsh.

The greater part of the Vale was retained by Fitzhamon and parcelled out to several of his vassal knights from which they would be expected to render knight's service. This included the obligation of following their lord to battle for forty days at their own expense. This was later commuted to money payments. They also had to provide a castle guard at Fitshamon's castle at Cardiff, which had become the headquarters of the Marcher lordship. Another duty was to attend the lord's monthly court in Cardiff, the "comitatus.' Unfortunately, the records of this court have been lost and, with them, a most valuable source of historical evidence. But this creation of what was called a "shire-fee" occupied by the knights who owed attendance at the comitatus court, was highly significant. It provided the nucleus of a structure which had characteristics of a shire long before the Tudor Act of Union created shires of the whole of Wales.

Outside this shire-fee, were established member lordships into which the rest of the Marcher lordships was divided. These were comprised of Llanblethian, Talyfan, Coity and Ruthin in the lowland (Bro) area and three others, Senghenydd, Miscin and Glyn Rothney (Rhondda) in the Blaenau or hill district, with a further three in the western portion of the lordship namely, Tir Iarll, Afan and Neath. The whole of the Blaenau region, from Afan to Senghenydd, remained in the hands of the descendents of Iestyn ap Gwrgant for over a century. The manor or lordship of Neath, established by Richard de Granville, was a dangerously sited, but strategically important, a frontier province flanked on the east by the Afan lordship from which many ferrocious attacks on Neath were to be launched in the years ahead.

Fitzhamon left for Normandy in 1105 and, at the seige of Falaise, was gravely injured by a spear wound in the head. After two years of agonising mental derangement resulting from this wound, he died in 1107. His body was brought back to England and buried at Tewksbury Abbey, where many of his descendants were also buried. This Abbey had been the recipient of many lavish gifts of Fitzhamon and magnificent effigies of some of the Marcher lords of Glamorgan (the Despensers) can be seen there today. After a period in royal custody, the lordship passed into the hands of Robert, King Henry's son, who acquired Fitzhamon's vast estates in England and Normandy as well as in Wales, through his marriage with Fitzhamon's daughter, Mabel. The bulk of his inheritance lay in Gloucester which, in 1122, was given earldom status. Robert, now Earl of Gloucester, became the most powerful magnate in the land.

The tomb of Hugh, Lord Despenser (d. 1349) and his wife Elizabeth Montague, in Tewkesbury Abbey.

The foundation charter of Neath Abbey has been lost but from copies of it, and from confirmation charters, it is clear that de Granville had, in 1129, granted to the monks of Saxigny, in Normandy, about ten square miles of rough land between the rivers Neath and Tawe, the Clydach and the Pwllcynon (Crymlyn) Brook. A confirmation charter to the Abbey by King John refers to the possession of the monks as "the place where Richard de Granville's castle once was". Evidently, the first castle, to which reference had already been made, was built west of the river. The more permanent castle, built on the east bank of the river where the present ruins stands, had obviously better defensive qualities, sited as it was on a steep sided river terrace with the Cadoxton marshes above and tidal marshes below. It was also, at the navigation limit of the river, a very important factor in the later commercial growth of the town.

A report on excavations carried out in 1963 by the Ministry of Works and promoted by the Neath Corporation suggest that, contrary to popular assumption, the castle, was initially, not a stone structure but of a somewhat similar type to the earlier earth and timber castle. Early in the 13th century, it was converted into a stone building with an oval curtain wall strengthened by rounded projecting towers. At high tide, the water, probably, came right up to the castle walls which would have enabled ships to sail up to a water gate. The first building on the east side of the river was probably, the work of Robert of Gloucester. De Granville, presumably, leaving no heirs, is recorded as leaving Neath, on the death of his wife,

North-west view of Neath Castle in County of Glamorgan by S. & N. Buck.
(By permission of the National Museum of Wales).

Constance, for his Devonshire estates. The story appears in Fuller's "Worthies of England" and it relates how Richard de Granville lived in Bideford "in great repute" in the reign of King Rufus. In his old age, he left for a pilgrimage to Jerusalem but he died on the journey. The account is untrustworthy for, of course, Rufus died in 1100, long before the foundation of the Abbey, but what appears certain is that de Granville was still alive in 1142 as his name appeared as a witness at a treaty between Earl Robert and Miles of Hereford in that year.

It was in this manner that the infant Neath Borough was born, in keeping with the formula of the marauding Normans who used the twin weapons of the castle and the Borough to ensure the establishment of urbanised settlements. In this way they sought to subdue, or at least contain, the hostile native Welsh in the surrounding countryside and to provide the castle with essential food and materials. They must have hoped that the planned security of such boroughs would attract settlers both English and Welsh just as they looked upon such places as potential sources of profit.

Neath was, therefore a garrison town and a planted borough. A Roman fort, Nidum, had been established half a mile to the west but there is no evidence of continuity between the departure of the Romans and the coming of the Normans and no real continuity of site. A few monastic cells and the royal village of the Welsh princes (Maerdref) at Briton Ferry could have no pretensions to any form of urbanised settlement. Indeed, the pastoral economy of the Welsh demanded none and there is very little evidence that the Welsh showed much interest in trade and commerce in pre-Norman times beyond some coastal trading in wool and hides. Along the coast there were probably small communities established by pillaging Norsemen in the 9th and 10th centuries judging from place names such as Swansea, Worm's Head, Laleston, Tusker and Flat Holm. Perhaps indeed, these footholds established by the Scandinavian sea rovers were an added encouragement to their Norman kinsmen to colonize this part of Wales.

CHAPTER 5

Neath Borough in the Middle Ages

Neath was amongst the first of the boroughs established by the Normans in Glamorgan; the others being Cardiff and Kenfig. These were followed in the early 13th century, by Llantrisant, Cowbridge and Caerphilly. To the east Chepstow (the first castle built on Welsh soil), Newport and Caerleon had been set up and, to the west, Swansea, Loughor, Laugharne, Carmarthen, Tenby and Pembroke were typical of a long line of borough settlements, all strategically situated to control the surrounding districts. It was not only greed for territorial possession which had motivated these Norman knights, but also, the political expediency of an attempted subjugation of the Welsh. The long tradition of border raids had shown the Norman kings the impossibility of national security in the face of an independent and rebellious Wales.

But what exactly was a borough? Domesday evidence indicates clearly that such places existed in Saxon times. It implied a fortified place although in many such settlements, there existed trading and commercial activities and, from the 10th century, boroughs of "burgs" emerges as distinct entities from the ancient shires and hundreds. In Wales, of course, there was no historical background of this sort. Outside the boroughts established by the Normans, were the tribal divisions of the Welsh commotes and cantrefs and many similarities with manorial organisations existed. But Welsh boroughs were, in the main, artificial creations. There was one distinctive feature common to them, and that was that the general character of the laws and customs was largely derived from the Norman 'bourg' of Bretuil, a small planned borough or bastide in Normandy founded by William Fitzosborn.

The borough towns of Wales had, therefore, to look to an obscure Norman stronghold as their legitimate parent. The liberties extended to the burgesses of Bretuil were extensive and attracted many settlers. The same privileges were granted by Fitzosborn to his boroughs in his Hereford territories and he was equally successful there. It was a natural and logical action and a recognition by the Norman lord of the value and

A stained glass portrait of King John from Cardiff Castle.

attractive urban centres in the peaceful penetration of newly conquered districts. The laws of Bretuil included specific grants of land within the "bourg", together with plots of agricultural land outside the walls. The possessing of these created the class of burgesses and the plots of building land were called burgages. For these burgages, a fixed annual rent of 12 pence was paid to the lord. The burgess enjoyed a free personal status and certain commercial privileges such as the right to trade in the market without payment of tolls but he was obliged to attend the lord's court where the civil and functional administration of the borough was carried out. The lord's profits were derived from trading tolls paid by non-burgesses and fines from the courts. These features were characteristics of the charter granted to most the Welsh boroughs by Earl William of Gloucester, who succeeded Earl Robert, in 1147, as the Marcher lord of Glamorgan. Cardiff was the first to receive such a charter as the capital of the lordship and it became a model for other charter grants.

It was, in this way, that Neath received her first charter from Earl William in about 1150. It was addressed to "his steward and Sheriff of Glamorgan and to all his Barons and ministers French, English and Welsh". In addition to the privileges described above, the burgesses were free to arrange the marriages of their sons or daughters without the permission of the lord. There was also no compulsion to bake their bread in the lord's oven or brew their ale in his brewery, and there were no dues payable for the filling or dyeing of cloth. But the fact that they were compelled to attend the court meant that, throughout the succeeding centuries, this was to grow with the increasing powers and privileges which were to be given them. Even so the first step had been taken in the release from the feudal restrictions which normally operated under the Norman manorial system.

It must be remembered, of course, that Neath, like so many other Welsh boroughs was never governed by a resident lord but by his officials. (The Mackworths, in the 18th century, never aspired to a feudal control). Through these, he kept the reins of political power. But in other respects, he was only too ready to absolve himself from the burden of administration. He encouraged the economic growth of the borough and thereby ensured his own income. To him these were one and the same thing. It was a case of power without obligation and profit without responsibility. As lord paramount of the Marcher lordship, he enjoyed almost royal power, for he held the lordship not of the king but by right of conquest. In the statutes appears the phrase "in the Marches where the king's writ does not run." The Marcher lords of Wales were, therefore, more powerful than the English lords. Apart from high treason, they had complete power over every kind of criminal or civil case. They could build castles, establish boroughs, grant charters, create forests and laws to govern them and declare and wage private wars. All fines, ransom goods of convicted felons and treasure belonged to them.

Their estates, however, reverted to the crown during the minority of heirs and this was to occur many times during the history of the Glamorgan Marcher lordship. It was not until the advent of Edward 1 that these powers were to be curtailed and then it was, largely related to the power of waging private wars. The king did not interfere with the internal administration of the lordship but, henceforth, he demanded feudal allegiance on the English pattern. More than one Marcher lord was to be taught a bitter lesson by Edward for acts of defiance. Prominent in such challenges to the king was Glamorgan's own lord Earl Gilbert (the Red) an exceedingly aggressive and power-motivated person who was not easily intimidated even by such a strong monarch as Edward.

Trouble had been fermenting for some time between Earl Gilbert and Humphrey de Bohum, Lord of Brecon. Raids and counter raids were carried out and the building of Morlais Castle on the border by Earl Gilbert (a great castle builder who built the greatest castle in Europe, Caerphilly) was the final irritant. The king decided that both earls needed a lesson, a very sharp one as a reminder of his authority. He struch hard. Both parties were ordered to appear before him at Abergavenny and were sentenced to heavy fines, imprisonment and the forfeiture of their estates. The mighty had fallen heavily. Having made his point, the King restored their positions but the Marcher lords throughout Wales had received a grim warning.

To return to the embryonic Borough of Neath, the picture emerges of nothing more than a fortified village, centred around the Castle. This was not simply a fortress. It was a place where all the administration of the borough was carried out, where the courts were held, the prison kept and where the Constable of the Castle and his garrison lived. The Welsh name for Neath, Castell Nedd, emphasized the total dominance of the castle in the early history of the town. The word "Nedd" itself is derived, according to Melville Richards, from an early form of Welsh word, Nida, which could mean "bright or shining", with reference to the river. The Romans, often, used the name of a river for their camps and the Neath Station was called "Nidum." A popular assumption is that Nedd is derived from "Nyth" (the Welsh for "nest") which could hardly be applied to a river. Dr Birch suggests that the word "Nid" or "Nedd" is the name for a river goddess which early settlers worshipped. Place names elsewhere such as Needwood and Needham and the River Nidd, suggest the same sacred origin. That the meaning is uncertain, is probably, the correct answer. The early anglicised form of Nedd was Neth or Nethe, later replaced by the modern "Neath" although, of course, many Welsh-speaking people speak of "Castell Nedd".

The Norman governing class would naturally speak French and their relatives French of English. There would be Welsh spoken by the natives who had either been taken prisoners or had chosed to join the settlement. To complete the language spectrum, all documents were, of course, written in Latin. The charter, with its reference to Welshmen, makes it plain that Earl William meant to encourage the native Welsh to integrate with the Borough which he was, obviously, anxious to develop into a functioning town.

No facts are available as to what type of manorial system structure had developed in this period of the middle of the twelfth century. Indeed, the Webbs are emphatic that no adequate knowledge exists as to what the manor was really like in its prime and what part the borough played in local government in this century. Nor, indeed, is there any documentary evidence of what life was actually like in Neath at this time. Charters and official documents are very limited in their information, but there must have been farming activities to provide food, and, just as obviously, there were craftsmen concerned with the necessities of living, the building of houses (most probably clay and watle with thatched roofs), the making of farm and military equipment, and the spinning and weaving of wool. In the local court, burgesses took an active part in administering law and order based on the simple patterns of "scot and lot" (the carrying out of obligations and the exercise of privileges).

Surrounding the settlement were extensive forests and undrained swamps where the wild boar, red deer and smaller creatures such as the otter and beaver lived. Hunting in the forests was, however, a jealously guarded aristocratic privilege and savage laws protected it. The ordinary settler could not even avail himself freely of any of the timber and had to wait for a much later charter for such rights.

It was sometime during this period that the church of St Thomas was built, almost certainly after 1173, since it was in the February of that year that Thomas a Beckett was canonized. The new church, near the precincts of the castle, was safer and more convenient than Llantwit church where the Normans previously worshipped, although records (dated 1262) tell us that the garrison had a chaplain to minister to them. His duties were confined to the castle and, for that reason, he was not allocated a horse, only an attendant. At that particular time, there were fifty persons in the garrison and thirteen horses. The town now had a castle-church nucleus. The dedication of the Church of St Thomas the Martyr was changed during the reformation to St Thomas the Apostle (Beckett was regarded by Henry VIII as a traitor) but the parish church continued to be at Llantwit until Elizabethan times.

Serious problems were now to face the borough, the chief one being the savage attacks periodically made by the native Welsh. The first recorded attack took place early in 1184, when Earl William died. Such onslaughts were almost invariably made on the death of a lord. This particular one was led by Caradoc ap Iestyn, lord of the neighbouring lordship of Afan but it was part of a general rising under the leadership of Rhys ap Gruffydd. The Afan territory had always been in Welsh hands and the Borough of Aberafan was the only borough in South Wales to receive a Charter from a Welsh lord, namely Leision ap Morgan Fychan (1283-1314). The Annals of Margam record that a band of Welshmen from the hill country attacked the Neath Castle but were driven off by the Normans or Frankcigene "who burned their seige engines". It is surprising that the Welsh had any military equipment of this kind (mechanical catapults) but, evidently, they had not yet developed the attacking techniques which they were to show, with such devastating effects, in later raids.

Towards the end of the century, local government structure had evolved to the stage of an early form of mayoral appointment. He was called Provost, by the name of Alfred. The real power was, of course, the Constable of the Castle, the representative of the lord. In the Pipe Rolls of 1184-85 quoted by Dr Birch, we learn that the Constable of the Castle was

Heraldic tile of the fourteenth century from Neath Abbey, showing the arms attributed to Robert, earl of Gloucester and lord of Glamorgan (d. 1147). It is now in the National Museum of Wales, Cardiff.

Walter de Cogan who had been appointed by the king for a period of six months for a payment of £10. Recent research has shown that officers such as de Cogan belonged to a "pool" and were appointed for definite periods whenever an administrative officer was required. These jobs could send them all over the country and even to Ireland or Gascony. It appeared, from the Pipe Roll, that relief to Neath was supplied by vessels carrying arms and food supplies. Payments are detailed for the services of knights of the Glamorgan lordship (such as William de Sor of Peterson, Walter de Lageles and Pagan de Turberville of Coity) and soldiers for strengthening the garrisons of Neath, Kenfig and other setlements during the Welsh attacks. One macabre item was 20 shillings for cord and timber which, it can only be surmised, was for the hanging of rebels.

After the death of Earl William, the Marcher lordship of Glamorgan, remained in the royal custody of King John, who visited Neath in 1220, on his way to Ireland and, again, on his return journey. After many complications relating to the inheritance of the lordship, it finally passed into the hands of a new ruling dynasty of Marcher lords, the de Clares.

The Rule of the de Clares (1218 to 1317)

The Lords of Glamorgan were all very powerful magnates, many of them important national figures. Gilbert de Clare, first of the de Clare dynasty, was not only the most powerful Marcher lord in Wales but also one of the biggest landowners in England. Throughout Gilbert's rule continual rebellions broke out until he organised all his forces and captured Morgan Gam, the lord of Afan, who was the chief trouble-maker. It was Morgan Gam who had, in 1224, raided Neath Abbey burning part of the buildings and killing 400 sheep.

De Clare died in 1230, but not before the Welsh rebel secured his release by delivering up hostages. Immediately, on the death of de Clare, the Welsh attacked. Llewellyn ap Yorwerth, Prince of North Wales, sparked off a revolt and aided by Morgan Gam, descended on Neath, overwhelmed the garrison and razed the castle to the ground with much slaughter of the inhabitants. It was at this time that Margam Abbey thought it advisable to pay "protection money" to the amount of £40 (quite a large sum in those days) to avoid being pillaged. Gilbert's successor was Richard de Clare, a boy of eight and it was not until 1240 that he was able to assume control of the lordship from the king's officers. Then he began the subjugation of the hill districts of the lordship (Blaenau Morgannwg) and the second stage of the conquest of Glamorgan was almost completed.

It was, probably, at this time that Neath Castle was rebuilt as a stone structure with, perhaps, stone walls protecting the township. A respite

Seal of Gilbert de Clare (d. 1230), earl of Gloucester and lord of Glamorgan and Newport. It is now in the National Museum of Wales, Cardiff.

from attacks allowed the building to be completed but, again in 1259, a strong band of Welshmen descended from the hill country, broke through the outer defences and burned the town dwellings right up to the castle walls. A mill and 150 houses were destroyed. Gilbert died in 1262 and the lordship passed into the King's hands and in the same year an official named Humphrey de Bohun was placed in charge and instructed to make a survey of the estates. And a melancholy state of affairs was revealed. Rents and tolls were much reduced and a reference to the large number of houses destroyed was made. A very significant item was that the survey was made under the oaths of a jury of twelve men, nine of whom bore Welsh names. By any standards, this suggests a substantial settlement of Welsh people in the borough. The Normans could be harsh to those who opposed them but, fundamentally, they were colonists anxious, for their own ends, to involve the native population in making a success of the boroughs they had established.

The tantalising scantiness of historical evidence means that we know very little indeed of the social and administrative lift of the town. No reference is ever made to women or children or to the extent of intermarriage. But what conflicting feeling there must have been in the minds of Welsh people in those days! To some, the temptation to accept the inevitable was great and, to live within the borough with its potential promise of a better standard of living and a set of privileges denied to those outside of a better standard of living and a set of privileges denied to those outside in the Welshery or "Patria". In others, a bitter hatred of an alien race of conquerors differing from them in race, culture and language was fanned by passions of revenge and, perhaps, a more materialistic urge to win booty from well-stocked castles. Life in the upland regions was undoubtedly tough and primitive. The very simplicity of their dress reflects this in the following lines:

"They be clothed wonder well
In a shirt, and mantell
A crysp breche well fayne
Bothe in wynde and in rayne
In this clothinge they be bold
Though the weder the ryghte colde
They doo fight, playe and lepe
Stonde, sytte, lye and slepe
Without surcot, gown, cote and kyrthe
Without lace and chaplet yn cappes
Without hode, hatte or cappes
And always with bare legges."

The Welsh soldiers, in the early Medieval times, fought barefoot with scarcely any armour. In one contemporary illustration, they are depicted

Heraldic tile of the fourteenth century from Neath Abbey, showing the arms of the de Clare family, earls of Gloucester and lords of Glamorgan. It is now in Swansea Museum.

with one shoe, probably in order to protect the foot when resting the lance or loading the bow. On the other hand, they were far better able to wage war, lightly clad in this way, in the hills and forests than the heavily armoured Normans. The latter had to develop new techniques of forest fighting before the northern part of the lordship was conquered.

As for national unity to combat the Norman, there was as yet little sign. Tribalism, the Welsh law gavelkind (by which inheritances were divided up amongst all the sons) and the fact that the separate Welsh kingdoms had been involved in the complex manoeuvres of conflicts between the English, Welsh and Norse for the past two centuries, hardly encouraged feelings of national unity.

In April 1280, the first grant of a fair was made to Neath by Gilbert de Clare. This was to be held on the day before the "Feast of St Margarets" (July 18) and was to last for three days, striking proof of de Clare's faith in the commercial potential of the town despite the ravages of war. How it had suffered is again indicated in the exchequer records of 1281. The rents of the mills ("burnt in the last war") were nil and the tolls off the fair were only 6 shillings described as "not more because of the war". Defaulting rents from the 150 houses destroyed in the last raids, show that none had been rebuilt and many others were in decay. Rents for coal (this is one of the earliest references to coal) and wood ashes were nil as there were no workers available. Other afflictions such as flooding by the sea or meadow land, meant no returns. Only fifteen acres were in use and these had been mowed for hay for the Sherriff's horses "against his coming to hold the court". Grim reminders appear in the accounts that law and order were being maintained. Expenses for hanging robbers amounted to 6 pence with 4 pence for ropes. Felony was an offence tried at the county court at Cardiff, for the sum of 2 shillings was paid for four men to take felons, Meuric ap Wranough and Meuric ap Howel Gam, to Cardiff.

At this time, the castle was being repaired and details appear in the accounts for wages paid to carpenters, masons and tilers and sums for the cost of lime, sand stones. The fact that they were paid wages for their work instead of such work being a feudal obligation arising out of tenure, indicates an advanced decay of manorialism in, at least, one of its aspects. Supplies of corn and animals from Pagan de Turberville to the Provost had been made to help out but of one consignment of corn, it was stated, "nothing remains". Kilthibebilth (Cily-bebyll) descried as a hamlet of Neath, had suffered particularly badly. Most of the tenants had been killed and their tenements laid waste. The three mills had been wholly destroyed in the war. As mills were essential for food, the picture was a very grim one, indeed.

The state records of 1296 tell us that one Walter de Hakelute had been appointed by the King as constable of the Castle at a yearly salary of £52 (to be paid by William de Caversham, Treasurer at Cardiff). Two years later, Robert le Norris appeared as Constable and Walter de Kachurens as Provost. There was still, however, no evidence of how the town was really governed but there were many charges of extortions and corruption against officials. In Neath, at this time, the family of Capenores were characteristic of this type. One of them, Stephen de Capenore, had succeeded Norris as Constable of the Castle and, with William Peres, the Provost, attested grants to Roger de Capenore in, at least, three parts of the town. Stephen Capenore himself, later, acquired thirteen burgages. This indicates a trend in estate building by greedy officials taking advantage of a market in land in troublesome times.

An even more significant example of the rapacity of the Capenores occurred in the hearing of a petition by the monks of Margam to the Sheriff of Glamorgan in 1329 at the Comitatus Court at Cardiff. The monks complained that they had suffered great hardship at the hands of the late Gilbert de Clare by the "advice and abetting of evil bailiffs and ministers". They had been dispossessed of estates in the hills of Kenfig and also of the Manor of Rossoulyn (Resolven) which had been granted to them by Morgan ap Caradoc, lord of Afan. The jury of twenty four included the current lord of Afan, John d'Avene. His family had married into Norman aristocracy and, by dropping the Welsh name of Afan, had adopted the name of d'Avene. The rebellious nature of John d'Avene's immediate ancestors, had very definitely been a thing of the past, he being now an arch-quisling. The petitioners succeeded in their plea and the

North-east view of Neath Abbey in County of Glamorgan by S. & N. Buck.
(By permission of the National Museum of Wales).

verdict of the lord, William La Zouch and his wife, Alianora (daughter of the late Earl Gilbert) restored to the monks all their lost possessions.

Gilbert de Clare (the Red), referred to above, had died in 1295. Six years previously, he had acquired extensive lands from Abbot Adam of Neath Abbey, which lay between the Nedd and the Tawe together with monastic lands at Briton Ferry. For these £100 in annual rents were to be

Map of Neath Abbey.

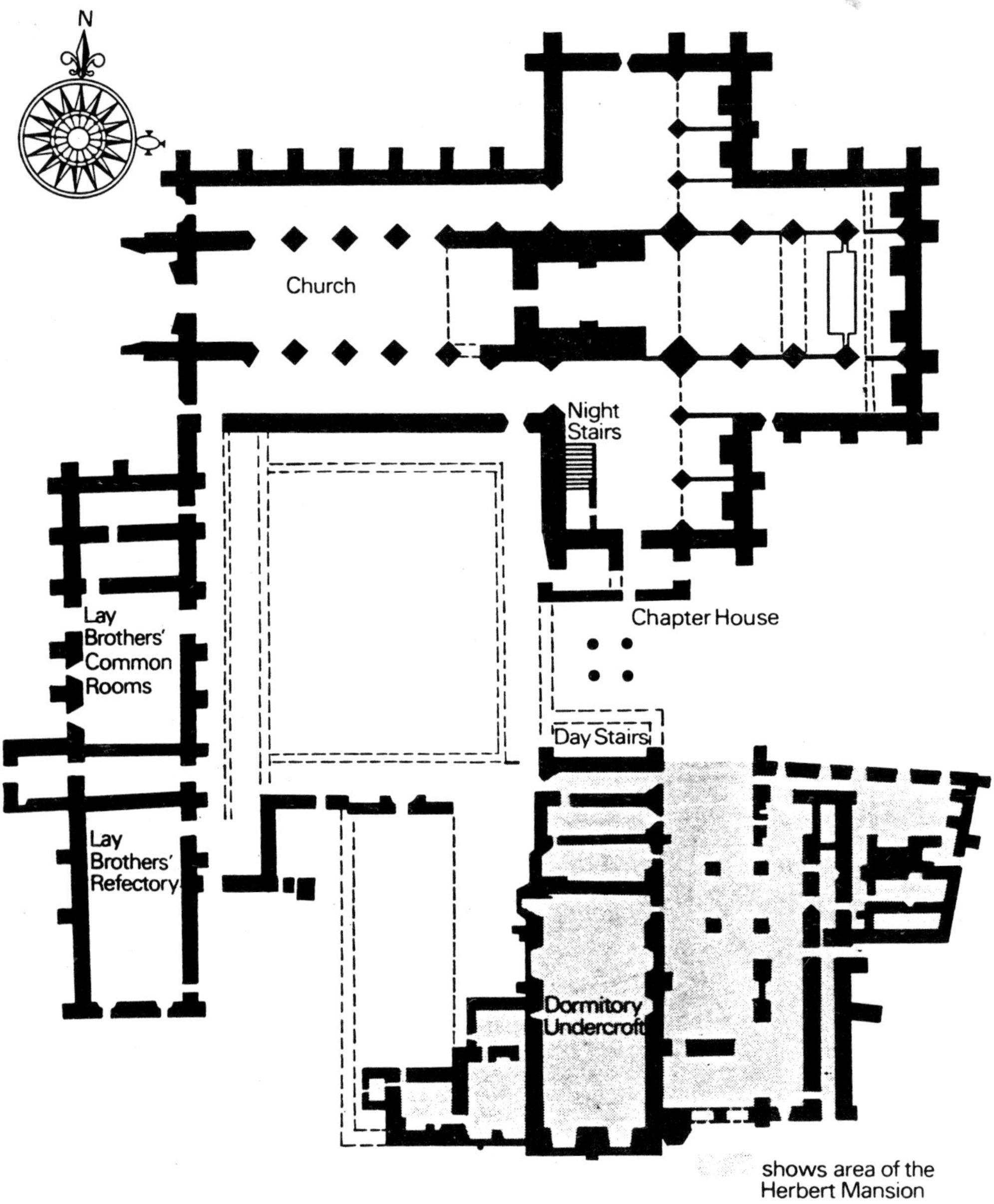

paid from properties in Neath, Cowbridge, Cardiff and Caerleon and the right to cut timber in the Earl's woods. Several reasons could be advanced for this action of the monks but no certainty exists; for the need for materials for a new church, income for the same purpose, trouble with their Welsh tenants or pressure from the aggressive Earl Gilbert. The last of the de Clares (1296-1314) was, despite his youth, a young man of great wisdom and ability. He occupied important positions under the Crown and established good relationships with the Welsh princes. He was tragically killed fighting the Scots at Banockburn, and, with his death, the age of the de Clares came to an end.

The thirteenth century had meant very little progress for the borough of Neath and at the end of the de Clare rule, it was one of the smallest of the Glamorgan boroughs. The century had seen many castles built and new boroughs had come into being such as Llantrisant, Cowbridge and Caerphilly. Administratively, the Marcher lordship had undergone reforms which made it a more efficient and cohesive unit. The next century was to see a new dynasty established, the Despensers, and, with it, an age of charters.

The Age of the Despensers

Between 1317 and 1413, the destiny of Neath was closely bound up with the rule of the Despensers, a family which was always deeply involved in the events of state. Some important charters were granted to the borough during this period which contributed much to the development of Neath. Yet this particular century could have hardly started worse than it did. After the death of the last de Clare at Bannockburn, the family estates were divided up between the late Earl's sisters. Immediately, the Welsh organised wide spread raids on the boroughs, always hated objects of attack. These occurred at a time when there was a general depression throughout the country and, indeed, across Northern Europe.

The period 1314-16 has been described as witnessing the gravest crises in the history of the Welsh boroughs. By the end of the year 1314, the greater part of Neath lay in ruins and, in the following year, the devastation was made even worse by the wide spread rebellion of Llewellyn Bren. But a combined effort by the Earls of Hereford and Brecon eventually smashed this revolt. Llewellyn surrendered at Ystradfellte Castle. Many of the rebels such as Rhys ap Gronow of Aberpergwm, Glynneath, were imprisoned but their leader was taken to Cardiff and there suffered the grisly, barbaric death of being hanged, drawn and quartered.

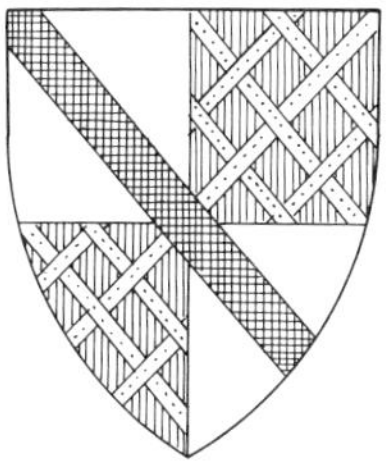

The Despenser Arms.

In 1322, there occurred the last recorded attack on Neath Castle. This time, however, it was by the baronial enemies of Hugh Despenser, King

Edward's new favourite. Despenser had succeeded to extensive estates, including the lordship of Glamorgan, by his marriage to Eleanor one of the co-heiresses of the de Clare inheritance. His accession to these estates was, however, bitterly disputed by the barons who already were on the verge of civil war against the King. Eventually, a baronial force, under Hereford, over-ran the whole of Glamorgan with much devastation everywhere, including Neath. The Castle was, once more, destroyed and the rebuilt or repaired castle is, most probably, the one which now stands in ruins today and which is now so energetically and skilfully being excavated and restored by the members of the Neath Antiquarian Society. (One of the interesting discoveries made was that of a cockpit in the centre of the courtyard. Cockfighting was a popular past-time of the castle residents.) The custodian of the castle, John Yweyn, was seized by the attackers and taken to Swansea where he and his servant, Philip Kerr, were hanged. Despenser, himself, was exiled but King Edward now roused himself from his customary inaction, gathered forces and defeated the rebel barons at Boroughbridge in the spring of 1322. Hugh Despenser was restored to his possessions and became the real power in the land. But his greed and rapacity eventually led to Civil War and Edward was deposed. Edward fled to South Wales with Despenser and, unsuccessfully, tried to escape to Lundy. Sheltering in Neath Abbey, the King was betrayed by the Welsh and was eventually captured at Llantrisant. He was later executed and Hugh Despenser met the same fate at Hereford. The lordship passed in 1288 to William la Zouche who married Despenser's widow in 1337; the lordship was once again in the possession of the Despensers, this time another Hugh Despenser, (son of the executed Despenser).

In 1331, financial accounts of the Steward and Provost of Neath, David Appeldoun, provides us with a few details of the borough. Rents from the town hall (the "bottehall") and a court called the hundred court were recorded but, generally, conditions showed little improvement. Although previously empty burgages had now found tenants.

Despite the slow progress throughout this century, there was a marked extension of burgess' privileges. Edward II had already granted, in 1324, freedom of tolls throughout the country to his favourite, Hugh Despenser and his burgesses. Later, in 1340, Despenser granted the burgesses special rights to forage for timber in his forests. These were described as "reasonable estovers" which meant timber and firewood for their homes and other requirements. This included "housebote" for building, "firebote" for fires, and "haibote" for fencing. The condition attached to these privileges was that there should not, in the opinion of the lord's foresters, be any waste or destruction of trees. It is surely astonishing that the burgesses had to wait for over a century and a half before they received privileges which

Opposite: Hugh Le Despenser II, from a stained glass window in Cardiff Castle.

were essential to meet basic elementary needs, especially when such extensive forests enveloped the countryside. The only explanation lay in the obsessive value the Normans placed on their forests. "They brought from Normandy their forests laws with lamentable results," writes Trevelyan, "of human suffering and servitude."

By the end of the twelfth century, sixty nine forests, almost a third of the country, belonged to the crown. Savage laws protected the royal privileges for the sole use of the forests for hunting. Poaching deer was punished by bodily mutilation under the Conquerer, William I, and under his successors even death was often meted out. In the Marches of Wales the forests, of course, belonged to the Marcher lords. No record of forest feudal laws survive but it is evident from the charters that privileges were not lightly given and it can be safely assumed that brutal punishments were the lot of any transgressor of the laws. It seems that hunting had declined during the fourteenth century but the lords recognised that the forests could provide a useful source of revenue. Very often the forests of non-resident lords were farmed out to foresters as they were almost certainly done in Neath. These officers received fees payable to them by users of the forests. Pannage, or the right to feed swine on the mast, yielded important dues whilst the sale of iron and coal was another source. A toll was exacted from all who kept hives in the forest but honey and wax from wild bees were always claimed by the lord. So were the much prized hawks and falcons. The foresters issued licences to craftsmen to make domestic utensils from selected timber to be sold later in the fair or market. All those cutting timber for whatever purpose, had to warn the forester of their presence, by three blasts on a horn or by striking a tree three times with an axe. But, with unsettled conditions, the decline in the numbers of deer, and the farming out of forests, these regulations gradually fell into disuse in the succeeding centuries. An interesting document survives (in the possession of the Neath Antiquarian Society) written by one Rees ap Jenkyn to whom the Neath Forest had been farmed out for one year (1483) in return for a payment of 40 shillings. The various dues which were once payable to the lord are described but, in the words of the account, "nothing is charged because all the aforesaid (dues) were let out to farm".

There were no monies received from trees blown down by the wind, from men making platters in wood, from licences to make wood ash and from coal and from iron. Neither were there any dues from licences to dig stones for tiles in the quarry of the lord within the forest of Glyndulais or dues from wild honey. Detailed reference to the pannage of pigs occurred. Pigs were allowed to feed in the forests in the autumn but, on St Martin's Day (November 11th), they were all rounded up by their owners. The foresters collected dues in money and in kind for the lord. Free tenants were supposed to pay 2 pence for each pig and bondsmen 1 pence. If any tenant had three pigs or more, one of the pigs had to be given to the lord. None of these dues was, however, forthcoming because all of them had been "let out to farm". Apparently, the forester was also excused the payment of tithes to the Rector of Neath "because they pertain to the farmer by agreement." The rent, 40 shillings was paid by ap Jenkyn to the Constable of the Castle, Thomas Huggerford, for transmission to the "Lord and Earl of Kerdyff."

In 1359, Neath was granted another charter which, together with that granted later in 1397, gave some positive direction to the future development of the borough. The policy of maintaining the exclusive character of burgess privileges was again emphasised by the regulation that all ships coming up the river to the port of Neath had to report to borough officials when they reached the "blackstone" (which marked the entrance to Neath harbour). This was a custom which in future years was to cause much friction between Abbey and town. This charter gave the first indication that Welshmen could enjoy burgess status although it was strictly confined to resident Welshmen. Restriction still operated in relation to pleas of the crown which could only be tried in the Sheriff's Court at Cardiff and certain other pleas in the county court. The Constable of the Castle held full power to hold the monthly court (an undifferentiated court, later to develop into the Court Leet and Court Baron) and also the Court of Pie Powder (from the French "pied-poudres" or dusty feet). This court dealt with all cases arising out of fairs and market days when people came from far and wide to sell or buy goods or just for entertainment. It was sometimes, called the "Wayfarers' Court" for obvious reasons. Market days and fair days must have been lonely and isolated in those days when communications were largely non-existent and what travel there was, was full of hazards. The weekly market dealt with local trading, involving, dairy produce, meat and wool. The three day fairs must have been the years big event when people on foot or with pack-horses thronged into the town.

We know that trading rules were tightly organised to ensure fair play for all including outsiders but that tolls were payable by all except burgesses. No details have come down to us regarding the merchants and the wares which they brought from other parts of the country but we can be sure that there were many goods displayed which excited the interest of the local inhabitants. Various entertainments, inseparable from fairs, must have taken place as elsewhere, jugglers, dancers, minstrels and the like. From early days, the magic of "The Fair" became deeply entrenched in the ethos of the town. And the magic is still there for many people.

Further advances in the development of the town resulted from the 1397 charter of Thomas Despenser. It confirmed, for the first time, the right of the burgesses to form a merchant or traders guild "at what time and whenever they wished for their own profit". Such guilds had existed in some Welsh boroughs for some time and were, of course, a feature of Medieval times. In such organisations the exclusive power of the burgesses in commercial activities operated. Normally, there was a council of 24 elected by the guild members. Wages, prices and profits were tightly controlled and non-members could only operate by payment of tolls and licences granted them by the Guild Council. Everyone had to obey the regulations otherwise they would find themselves in the stocks. In some places certain crafts would develop guilds of their own. In Cardiff, there was a Cordwainers' Guild (Shoemakers) with its own Guild Hall. Guild organisations were, in effect an association of producers (to use a phrase of the Webbs) and this description could very well apply to what boroughs were really like in their structure and the manner of operation. As well as confirming the three day fair of the "Holy Margaretta" granted back in 1280, another four day fair was included beginning on the Feast of Corpus Christi. The weekly market "on the day of the moon" was also confirmed at Neath.

Exclusive to the burgess was the right to cut turf for the hearth, rushes for the floor and stones for building. Anyone who was not a burgess caught doing this would be summoned to the monthly court. In view of this, it is difficult to see how anyone outside the burgess class could live with any degree of comfort of any kind. Second class citizens would be a flattering term to apply to them. Even more remarkable was that this restriction prevailed for several centuries. In a seventeenth century Court Leet, a widow was presented for cutting turf, for which offence she was fined.

The lord retained tight political control of the borough through his representative, the Constable of the Castle, who was the real power in the town. He presided over the hundred court and the Court Pie-Powder. Local jurisdiction received a further extension of power in that all offences relating to public disturbances, theft and debt could all be tried in the local court ("Le Courthouse"). The exception was treason, reversions of land and conspiracies. A prison was to be kept for the "castigating and guarding of all prisoners" and for the carrying out of executions in the presence of the Constable of the Castle. The latter was described for the first time as "mayor of the town." Peculiarly enough, this was the one and only use of this term until the Municipal Reform Act of 1835. For the privileges granted them, the burgesses paid an annual unspecified sum. An important right of the burgesses was that they now had the power to elect a bailiff or reeve themselves.

The century had, however, despite the charters, seen very little development in the size of the borough. Revolts and plagues had been extremely destructive. The Black Death struck in 1348-9 and, again, in 1361 and 1369, and great havoc and distress was caused. Although the visitations of the pestilence in Glamorgan were not so severe as in other parts of Wales, the effects were serious.

What seems evident was that Neath, at the end of the century, had developed considerable trading both by sea and land. Craftsmen, too, were much in evidence. Each burgage tenement inluded a plot of ground in front of the house (usually seven feet long) with a garden at the back. The front room of the house was normally a combined workshop and living room where utensils were made and sold. Each craftsmen would naturally specialise in one commodity and surplus articles in wood, leather, iron and cloth would be exchanged. The room at the back of the house served both as a kitchen and bedroom for the whole family. Two storey houses would have the bedroom on the upper floor. As a burgess, he could keep a malt house and an oven which were probably accommodated in lean-to additions. Very few people could read, so a sign had to be placed outside each shop or workshop. Alehouses, usually kept by a woman, had a bunch of twigs attached to a pole outside. Everyone was expected to hang a lantern outside the door at night and also keep the road outside his dwelling free of refuse. Despite all disasters, the natural resilience of people ensured that life in the borough went on and there were naturally many moments in the daily round when there were pleasures to be enjoyed.

The century ended disastrously for the Despensers. In 1400, Thomas Despenser, the benefactor of the 1397 charter, was executed for treason having joined forces within a conspiracy to restore the deposed Richard II to the throne. Thomas, his father, Edward, and his uncle, Hugh, had been deeply involved in national events. Edward had fought in the Irish Wars and at Crecy with contingents of the famous Welsh bowmen. He died in 1349 and was buried at Tewkesbury Abbey where his magnificent tomb is one of the glories of English sculpture. Edward, his nephew and successor, fought with the Black Prince at Poitiers in 1356. In 1370, he was in Italy, supporting Pope Urban in his war against Milan. It is thought that he appeared in the fresco painted by Andrea da Firenze in the Church of St Maria Novello in Florence. The painting depicts the meeting of Pope Urban and the Emperor Charles IV in October 1368. Edward died at his Llanblethian manor house at the age of 39 and was buried, as were so many Glamorgan Marcher lords, in Tewkesbury Abbey. He was a typical soldier baron of Medieval chivalry and was described by Froisart as the most handsome, most honourable and most courteous knight of his time.

But Neath, like many other Glamorgan boroughs, received little personal attention from the Despensers apart from the granting of Charters and, it must be remembered, that these grants were a profitable business to them. They spent little time in the lordship although the disappearance of most of the Despenser records makes it difficult to be positive about it.

The Age of the Warwicks

In the early fifteenth century, the lordship of Glamorgan passed into the hands of the Beauchamps through the marriage of Isobel Despenser, a posthumous child of the traitor, Thomas Despenser, to Richard Beauchamp, Earl of Warwick. Eventually, the earldom passed to Richard Neville, Earl of Salisbury and Warwick, who became known as Warwick the King-maker and the leading figure in the War of the Roses. The Battle of Bosworth ended the line of the Warwicks and, with the accession of Henry VII, the lordship was awarded, along with other extensive estates, to his uncle Jasper, Duke of Bedford. The Medieval period of the Marcher lords was, virtually, at an end.

How had Neath borough fared this century of national turbulence? Again, it is largely a melancholy story. The fifteenth century had showed a steady decline in the fortunes of most of the Welsh boroughs. Neath, at the end of the century, had shown a sharp drop in market tolls and rents. In 1491, the Bottehall was in ruins, stretches of meadow land had, repeatedly, been flooded by the sea; the only income of any consistency was from the local courts, and William Rees makes it clear that the effects of the Glyndŵr Rebellion early in the century had been far more devastating than even the plagues had been in the preceeding century.

The privileged boroughs had been special objects of attack, since the trade of the county had been regulated in the interests of the burgesses of the towns and officials had been harsh in the exaction of revenues from the Welsh districts. Many Welshmen had gained experience of warfare whilst fighting in France and systematic destruction had devastating effects for many decades. Neath Castle seems only to have survived due to its strong garrison of a hundred archers and thirty lancers.

Boroughs such as Llantrisant and Caerphilly, had declined markedly towards the end of the century and Kenfig's hope of recovery was completely blighted by sand encroachment. Aberafan, also, suffered from advancing sand and sea which made much of its land worthless. Jasper, Duke of Bedford, like so many other of the Marcher lords seldom, if ever, visited South Wales. The administration of the lordship was largely left to Morgan Kidwelly, a lawyer of outstanding capablitities who had served as

Bronze effigy of Richard Beauchamp (d. 1439), earl of Warwick and lord of Abergavenny and Glamorgan, in St Mary's Church, Warwick. Courtland Institute of Art, University of London.

Bedford's Counsellor and Chancellor of Glamorgan. The Duke of Bedford died in 1495 and the lordship eventually passed into the hands of the King's relative Sir Charles Somerset, on a seven year lease from the King at a heavy rent of 1,000 marks (a mark was worth 68 pence). He, also, became Sheriff of Glamorgan, but Henry demanded a bond of £3,000 to ensure that he did something to curb the widespread lawlessness in the country at that time. He was created Earl of Worcester in 1514 and on his death in 1526 was succeeded by his son, Henry, Earl of Worcester.

Over four centuries had passed since Neath had been established on the banks of the Nedd as a garrison town and profound changes had taken place in its character as a borough. The whole of the lordship of Glamorgan was now under unified control with the Welsh completely subjugated. The castle had lost any reason for its existence. The period of the Middle Ages could, in one sense, be described as the birth and the death of the castle. It spanned a period as great as that which lay between Queen Elizabeth I and the present day yet the actual physical growth of the town was limited to a few streets surrounding St Thomas Church with a market situated between the Castle and the Church as a focal point of commercial activity. The existence of the port had enabled a sea trade to develop as early as the thirteenth century, an activity which led to a bitter quarrel between the monks and the burgesses of the town. A petition to the King in 1521 led to an inquiry by the Earl of Worcester. The result of this was that the trading monopolies of the town, which had been threatened by the Abbey, were restored.

The growth of the town had not proceeded on the basis of such a carefully planned layout as in some of the North Wales towns such as Flint, Conway and Rhuddlan. Yet there was, according to Harold Carter, the elements at least, of a planned medieval town. In the future years, the development of the boroughs in Wales would depend on what natural economic resources they possessed now that their significance as garrison towns had disappeared. Those towns which possessed no such resources decayed. Others, like Neath, survived and grew. Perhaps, one of the main factors was her sea trade and the development of her coal industry. Leland, the antiquary, noted of Neath, that "the little town and castelle of Neath standith 4 miles from the mouth of the Neth . . . there cummith up Shippletes almost to the town of Nethe from the Severn. Botes cum to the very bridge of tymbre that is somewhat lower on the water than the town."

Despite quarrels about trade between the Abbey and the town, the inhabitants of Neath must have been fortunate in having the Abbey so close at hand during the past centuries. It must have been an invaluable compensatory factor, in view of the disasters throughout the Middle Ages. It is true, of course, that the abbey was not immune from troubles which afflicted the town, but, generally, it enjoyed a far more favourable existence. It had meant more to the community than a place of devotion and contemplation, vastly important as that was in an age of violence and insecurity; to the sick and the old and to the outcast, it had been a haven of rest and succour. To those who sought learning and scholarly dedication, it was here that they found it. Such was the highly skilled nature of the monks' farming techniques, that the employment of lay brothers (the "conversi") not only provided employment for the local inhabitants (and casual labour for those who needed it), but also the opportunity to learn brilliant methods of husbandry in all its aspects; and, just as surely, they must have benefitted from commercial activities in sea trading and mineral works.

It is true that the Abbey, prior to its dissolution in 1539, had declined in

Neath Abbey. The remains of the abbey church, principally the walls of the nave and the west front.
(By permission of Eagle Photographers).

influence. Eventually, its personnel had dwindled to an abbot and seven monks. But it had never laid itself open to the charge of corruption to which other monasteries had. Indeed, a short time before its end, Lewis Morgannwg (the leading Welsh poet of his day) had sang its praises in lavish terms which, allowing for a measure of hyperbole, indicated the high reputation the Abbey enjoyed. This was why, probably, that the Abbot Leyson, himself a greatly respected figure, was granted a pension of £40 and the monks received one varying from £3.6s.8d. to £4 a year. But, undoutedly, the monasteries had outlived their usefulness and the end of Neath Abbey was not accompanied by any cry of protest from anyone. Lewis Morgannwg was soon to sing the praises of the monarch who had destroyed the monasteries and even Catholic squires were quick to buy up monastic estates without any compunction. It was one of the many signals which heralded the end of the Middle Ages.

Administratively, the borough had developed a substantial element of municipal structure with a Portreeve, Aldermen and a council of burgesses. The stage was now set for a new epoch in local administration with the passing of the Act of Union. But as yet, in terms of population, the town had little more than 500 people.

Henry VII from a stained glass window in Cardiff Castle.

CHAPTER 6

Neath under the Tudors and Stuarts

When Henry Tudor defeated Richard III at Bosworth, it was the Standard of Wales, with a red dragon on a white and green background which had been hoisted in battle and it was that which accompanied him on his triumphal march to London. Welshmen all over Wales had ensured his victory after the historic march from Milford to Bosworth and Henry was not slow to acknowledge the fact.

The previous century had been a dismal period for the Welsh people. After the crushing defeat of the Glyndŵr Rebellion, severe penalties had been enforced on the Welsh and a period of demoralisation had set in only relieved by the poetic utterances of the bards. A bitter hatred pervaded their writings but also stirring prophecies of how, one day, a saviour would arise and restore, not only the ancient independence of the Welsh nation, but also supremacy over the English. And now with a monarch of Welsh blood on the throne, the bardic prophecies were fulfilled. Or so they believed.

The truth was, that the King, preoccupied as he was with the problem of establishing national unity out of chaos, had little time for anything practical for Wales. However, he did bring into being an instrument of government called the Council of Wales and the Marches (first mooted by Edward IV) and this court played a vital part in judicial administration in Wales for over a century.

It was his gifted son, Henry VIII, and his brilliantly able minister, Thomas Cromwell, who were responsible for legislation which transformed the situation in Wales, and began a new era in its history. Laws which were enacted during the period of 1536-42 (under the generic name of the Act of Union) brought to the Welsh people the same rights and laws generally that were enjoyed by the people of England.

Wales, in fact, became integrated with England. The royal jurisdiction of the Marcher lords was abolished and the whole of Wales divided up into shires. To the lordship of Glamorgan was added the lordship of Gower and Kilvey, thus bringing into being the modern county of Glamorgan.

Parliamentary representation was granted to Wales but, unlike the English shires which had two members, the Welsh shires were granted only one, probably to save them expense. Neath was grouped with seven other boroughs in Glamorgan (Cardiff, Cowbridge, Llantrisant, Aberafan, Kenfig, Swansea and Loughor) to return a burgess to Parliament, the right of voting being a privilege of each burgess owning property of £2 annual value. It is beyond the scope of this work to deal in any depth with the Act of Union legislation but mention must be made of the appointment of county justices and a system of courts called the Quarter Sessions. This court, and the J.P.s who operated through it, were to play an immensely important part in the civil as well as the judicial administration of the county until the separation of these two functions by the 1888 Local Government Act. In the eighteenth century it was, undoubtedly, to become more important, as a local government body, than the parish or the borough.

The position of the Welsh gentry was considerably strengthened by this Henrician legislation. Benefitting from the changes of landownership, resulting from the Dissolution of the Monasteries in 1536 and 1539. they became a powerful class from which the Justices were inevitably drawn and they were to dominate the county administration for centuries to come.

There was, of course, one serious blemish in the Act of Union. It debarred anyone holding public office from using the Welsh language. Henry's object of achieving national unity meant not only political and legal integration, it involved cultural assimilation as well. It is doubtful, however, whether this penal clause did or could operate in the way it was intended. The severe legal restrictions from settling in town imposed on the Welsh people after the Glyndŵr rebellion now disappeared and there was an influx of Welshmen into many of the towns (from rural areas). Dyfnallt Owen has pointed to the cymricisation of the urban areas as one of the far reaching effects of the Act of Union. "The newcomers lost no time in qualifying for various crafts and professions and infiltrated into the most influential municipal posts."

In actual fact, however, evidence exists as far as Neath is concerned that this process of cymricisation had been going on for a considerable time. One of the reasons for the Act of Union was to exact taxes from the people of Wales. The collection of the Exchequer subsidy was based on the hundreds, created out of the ancient Welsh "commotes", and a detailed list of taxes collected from householders in 1543 survives from the "Hundredum de Nethe." It shows that the names, with very few exceptions, are Welsh including those of the collectors. One of the officials, Ieuan Llwyd, had occupied the position of Portreeve of the town as early as 1521, the period when Sir Rice Mansel of Margam was Constable of the Castle. Neath and all the other parishes making up the hundred could, therefore, be described as thoroughly Welsh. Evidently, the penalties imposed on the Welsh people after the Glyndŵr Rebellion had been allowed to lapse (although still remaining on the statute book). Incidentally, the only name that echoed the Norman past was that of James Frensheman.

Many Welshmen, seeking wider fields of activity after the Union, flocked to London and distinguished themselves in many fields. One English writer who acknowledged this was Ben Johnson in his masque "For the Honour of Wales," in which the King was addressed as follows "What lights of learning hath Wales sent forth for your schools? What industrious students of your laws? What able ministers of your justice? Whence, hath all the Crown in all times, better servitors, more liberal of their lives and fortunes?"

What can be said of the internal administration of the borough at this time? Fortunately, the powers invested in the borough found expression in 1542, in the issue of Ordinances of the town made by the Constable, Portreeve and Burgesses. They provided a set of by-laws which give a much sharper picture of the town than was previously available and indicate quite clearly that a "close" corporation of nominated and adopted members operated in controlling the social and economic life of Neath.

Consumer protection interests operated markedly in those far-off days, especially in relation to the quality and price of bread. Bakers were forced to bake "good and holsome bread" in loaves of two sizes (one loaf for 1 penny and two small ones for 1 penny). This, it was stated, was to conform to the "assize" a very old law to ensure the quality of bread baked and ale brewed. All commercial activities, down to the last detail, were controlled tightly in the interests of the burgesses. Cargoes on ships entering port were to be examined by two burgesses with specialised knowledge of particular cargoes. Such commodities were then open to purchase by the burgesses according to their needs. Non-burgesses could, presumably, buy what was left.

The proceedings were controlled by a "jury of six" which was in the nature of an inner council. The exclusive right of market trading were jealously guarded. Anyone selling goods before they came on the market were fined as was anyone caught "cornering the market" in any commodity. The wool trade was also very important at that time and the buying and selling of cloth was confined to fair days. No-one could buy "Welsh cloth, white Russet or Blacke" or any type of yard, within the town except on fair days.

The protection of the town and its property, the prevention of public nuisances and of "fighting and brawling" were all matters of concern to the town authorities. An obligation was placed upon every inhabitant to defend the town and its officials which meant that a resident had to keep "defencible weapons and harnesse after his abilities." Fighting seemed to have been a popular pastime in Tudor times and an attempt was made to control it. Anyone drawing blood was fined ¾p and others were fined "as it should please the Constable of the Castle and the Portreeve." The position of the Council and its officers was safeguarded against conspiracies, by punishments of imprisonment in the town gaol and substantial fines. The ducking stool or, as it was called the "Cooking Stoole," received special mention. Any woman who "doe scolde or rage against any Burgess or his wife or any other person and his wife," and who was found guilty by the jury of six men, was sentenced to sit one hour on the "Cooking Stoole;" for the second offence for two hours and, for the third, it was a case of "to let slip the pyn" which meant a ducking. One can only hope that this did not take place in the brook which ran down Water Street from the Gnoll and which, probably, was in the nature of an open sewer. Most probably, it was in the town pond which was situated opposite the main entrance to the Castle ruins as shown in old maps.

Intermarriage between Welsh and English had long been taking place and, as we have seen, the Welsh had, by this time, become dominant in the town. Yet it was laid down that any burgess having a Welsh wife who threatened her neighbours with action against them by her friends or kindred, would be fined on being found guilty by the "jury of six," and so would her husband. Obviously, the council was determined to prevent any incitement to relatives living outside in the "Welshery" to participate in quarrels inside the town.

The defensive attitude of the council was reflected not only by the exclusiveness of the commercial privileges; it was echoed in the restriction imposed on the freedom of speech. The ordinances enacted that anyone saying "any unfitting words which would be rebukeful or spiteful to the portreeve or council or against the good rule of the town would be subject to a fine of six shilings and eight pence." It could also be seen in the bye-law, which forbade any inn-keeper to give lodgings to any stranger coming into the town on horseback or on foot. The tight control on the admission of burgesses was a reflection of the same attitude. The ceremony of admission took place in the Guildhall (which stood in the present Old Market Street). There the portreeve and the Council assembled and "discreetly and without partiality" examined the applicant as to his worthiness to become a burgess, the chief qualification being a willingness to be obedient to the Portreeve and the council! It is significant that the Constable of the Castle was not included in the ceremony.

What plainly emerges is that a high degree of local autonomy by the Portreeve and senior members of the council had been established. The lord's man, the Constable of the Castle, had ceased to be the real ruler of the town as he had been for so long. The lords of Glamorgan had been shorn of their royal jurisdiction by the Act of Union but they were now prepared also to further shed the burden of local administration within the borough, and to enjoy what profits they could exact from the burgesses arising from ancient dues which the Act of Union had allowed them to keep. A high water-mark of local independence had been reached and the corporation was to develop almost as it pleased.

Elizabethan Neath was, therefore, a town which had substantially recovered from the disasters of the previous century. The Guildhall had replaced the Castle as the administrative centre of the town. This building, sited in the present Old Market Street, also contained the market on the ground floor. It was no longer Castell Nedd in the sense of a Castle-nucleus town, although the number of streets was limited to about eight in the proximity of Castle and the Church. In an inventory of a sale of chantry lands in 1557, the following streets are mentioned, Shipman Strete, Olde Strete, La New Strete (Cattle Strete), Highe Strete, Gilden Strete (Gold Strete), Water Strete, Wyn Strete. A plan of Elizabethan Neath shows the general layout of the town. Although no direct evidence is available, it can be reasonably assumed that Neath shared in the general rise to a more civilised way of life than in the pre-Tudor times. In the better-off homes, feathers replaced straw beds and carpets for rushes on the floors. Wines as well as beer and cider would be drunk, eating vessels were of pewter and clothes would be of richer and more varied colours. Almost every house had a garden where fruit, vegetables and a variety of herbs were grown.

Neath, which was referred to at this time as a "Borough and Manor", had member-manors which made up the lordship of Neath. The manor of Neath Ultra and Cilybebyll occupied the area between the Nedd and the Tawe which was, largely, land bought from the Abbey by Gilbert de Clare in 1289.

Neath Citra and Briton (Ferry) comprised a peculiar "horseshoe" shaped manor from St Illtud's Brook, the upper Cimla to Cryddan Brook and Sart Ditch to the river. The manor of Cadoxton had always been part of the Abbey lands. It was made up of a territory extending from Aberdulais to Crymlyn Bog. At the dissolution of the Abbey in 1439, its site and demesne (lord's) lands, were leased to Sir Richard Cromwell (a relative of Thomas Cromwell and formerly of a family called Williams of

Lanishen). Cadoxton passed to Sir George Herbert of Swansea in 1545 and, later, this family acquired all the Abbey lands.

Very little is known how Neath Ultra and Citra were administered. They formed part of the lordship of Neath under the Crown. The lordship was sold by Queen Elizabeth, in 1560, to William Herbert, Earl of Pembroke, together with the monastery of Llantarnam, for £3,199. sixteen shillings and six pence farthing. In later documents Briton Ferry was regarded as seperate from Citra, for we find that, in 1601, Philip, Earl of Pembroke, held Neath Burgis, Neath Ultra and Cilybebyll, Neath Citra and Briton. Neath Ultra was, of course, the Welshery or Patria of Neath where Welsh tenures and customs had been allowed to continue on payment of rents to the lord. Manorial courts (which the Act of Union legislation allowed to survive) were held, in particular, the Court Baron or lord's court.

The feudal dues and rights which the Lord Marches had retained, despite the 1536 Act, were further relinquished in 1612 by the Earl of Pembroke but only at a price. The grant provides a clear picture of the amount of restrictions which had still been operating at that time. A number of parcels of Common Land was released to the burgesses at Cefn Saeson, Westernmoor, the upper and lower Latt, the Mera, the town hall (Guildhall), the assize of bread and ale, pitching, keelage and anchorage dues and all coal dug on the aforesaid lands. But the lord still reserved several seignorial dues such as the goods of felons, estrays, wrecks and the right to use the town hall for the execution of any business by the Earl or his family and heirs. For the various privileges granted, the burgesses were required to pay £20 and a yearly rent of £6. thirteen shillings and fourpence, together with 6 pence for every "wey of coales" dug on the lands mentioned and exported. The Portreeve was expected to collect these dues at a yearly audit. Any failure to collect would result in a distraint of burgesses' goods and levy of a £5 fine.

A survey of the Borough Liberties of Neath made after the Restoration in 1666 on behalf of Philip, Earl of Pembroke, was largely a recital of the grants of 1612. Mention was made of a payment of £4. ten shillings payable by the borough on the death of the lord. This was an ancient feudal due called "mises" which the lord, seemingly, was determined to retain. This payment related to the number of cattle possessed which resulted in the manor of Neath Ultra and Cilybebyll having to pay £57. two shilling and seven pence and Neath Citra £22. seventeen shillings and two pence. Another very ancient seignorial due was the payment of "heriots" on the death of a free tenant or copyholder or on the passing of his land to a new tenant, the payment of 5 shillings, due to the lord. This feudal exaction survived astonishingly, until 1928, when a notice of a scale of property in Kaegurwen Manor (Gwaen Cae Gurwen area) contained the condition that a "heriot" would be payable. The picture is of a town which was almost completely autonomous but exhibiting little concern for any responsibility for the wider needs of the community. There appeared to be no organised book-keeping or record keeping of the administration. The borough had, in fact, decayed, markedly, as a unit of local government.

Proceedings at a Court Leet held in August 1677, before Sir Herbert Evans, Constable of the Caslte, and David Leyshon, Portreeve, showed a very limited desire to serve the community. A certain William Phillips and fifteen others were fined for resisting the action of the Portreeve, Common Attorneys, Haywards and several burgesses, in turning away animals belonging to the defendant from town lands. Others were fined for not scouring a brook and for "turning a stream to the great annoyance of the inhabitants." A former Recorder of the borough, Hopkin David, was fined for not delivering up to the Court the lord's records belonging to the town. At a court holding the following year, the obligation of the inhabitants to repair the river bridge was instanced when a fine for the neglect of this work was levied. At a further court, held in 1679, fines were levied on individuals for selling goods under weight, for encroaching a common land, for not repairing highways (which meant little more than filling up potholes) and for several instances of failing to scour brooks. Breaking the town stocks was another offence which was recorded. A popular sport at that time, especially on festival and fair days, was bull-baiting. Anyone who failed to bait his bull and sold the beef of a bull "not being baited" was summoned to the Court Leet. The bull ring was sited in Glamorgan Street. A house in New Street (Cattle Street) was called the "Bull-ring House."

The obligation to serve in various offices was often resisted by the burgesses, especially that of the Petty Constable whose duties of enforcing law and order over his neighbours in this small community would be liable to cause resentment. One of the Petty Constables, a Williams Thomas refused to "set watch and ward" at the instructions of the Portreeve. The Constable was reported as having said indignantly that the Portreeve "was fitter to be in the stocks than himself." The duties of constables, which residents were obliged to take on, based on a street rota system, were certainly onerous. It included searching neighbours houses for the carcases of stolen animals, a very prevalent offence. The duties of "watch and ward" seem to have been of two kinds. One was concerned with patrolling the streets at night to maintain peace and order. A special concern was to prevent any unauthorised strangers entering the town under cover of darkness. The other duty was that of dealing with cattle and sheep thieves in the fields outside the town. A watch was kept on Drymma mountain for this purpose. It was the duty of the constable to organize a meeting at the Latt, where weapons were stored ready to be distributed to those whose turn it was to keep watch. In a Court Leet held in 1684, there was recorded a case of thee Petty Constables fined for neglecting their duty of organizing "watch and ward" between sunset and sunrise. At the same court, two residents were fined for disobeying a constable's instructions in connection with this duty. One of the defendants was, incredibly, a woman. The people were, apparently, of the mind that the ducking stool was no longer in favour for it had been allowed to fall into disrepair. The jury of the court, however, thought otherwise and ordered the inhabitants to provide one. Was it possible that some of the jury had scolding wives?

The same resistence to community laws was shown by tavern keepers. Several were recorded as having been guilty of resisting the efforts of the borough's two ale-tasters to ascertain the quality of the ale brewed. Two people from Cadoxton were fined for selling bread in the market under the lawful weight. No fewer than nineteen people were fined for selling ale without a license and for selling ale under measure (less than a quartt for one penny).

This twice yearly held Court Leet was a place where almost any business relating to minor offences or property rights could be dealt with. It was in such a court that residents of the borough would:

"Impeach a broken hedge
And pigs unringed, at Vis Franc Pledge,
Discover thieves, bawds and recusants.
Tell who did play at games unlawful
And who filled pots of ale but half-full."

The collection of Hearth Tax was one of the most onerous and often dangerous duties of the King's officers. Several people were presented at court in 1686 for assaulting these officers with weapons. Three of the accused held offices of Petty Constables of the town.

It was about this time (approximately 1686) that Neath received its last charter. The Tudors consistently adopted a policy of supporting borough governments but one of the vices of the Stuarts was a gross interference in local government affairs. Under Charles II, the attack on the Boroughs commenced by depriving London of its franchise and all its privileges because its loyalty to the Court was suspect. Under his successor, James II, charters were confiscated because of opposition to Roman Catholicism. A state of panic was created. Many towns, including Neath,

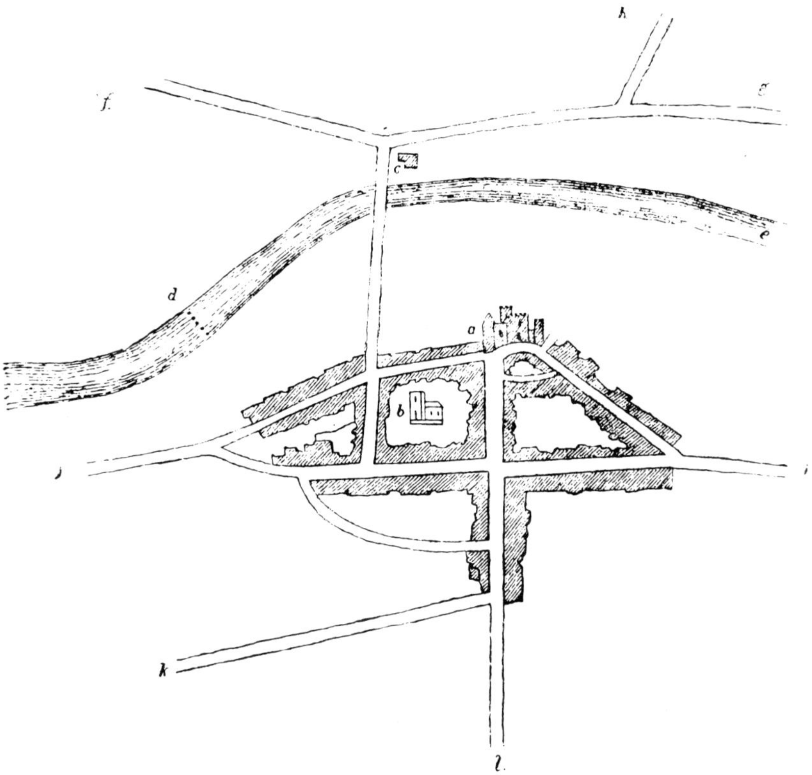

Neath in the days of Queen Elizabeth (about 1600).

a. The Castle.
b. St Thomas's Church.
c. St Giles's Chapel.
d. The old Abbey Weir.
e. The River.
f. The Abbey Road.
g. The Cadoxton Road.
h. The Pen-y-wern Road.
i. The Llantwit Road.
j. A road to the Millands.
k. The Briton Ferry Road.
l. The Road to Pontrhydyfen.

were induced to surrender their charters. But, with the landing of William of Orange imminent, James hastily restored most charters to court popularity, but under the guise of Royal magnanimity. Hence, the Neath Charter.

Under the terms of this Charter, it was made clear that Neath was now to be an incorporated borough. This meant "that they (the Reeve, Alderman and Burgesses) and their successors hereafter and forever shall be, by force of these presents, one body corporate and politic in deed, in fact and name . . . and, by the name, they have perpetual succession."

The question whether a borough was incorporated or not was always in difficult one and a perpetual source of argument with legal historians. The Webbs maintained that incorporation meant the creation of a fictitious person as a legal entity having perpetual succession, and this could only be granted by a Royal Charter. Weinbaum suggests five conditions which incorporation demanded, namely the possession of lands, a common seal, authority to issue bye-laws, perpetual succession and the power of being sued or tu sue as a whole by the specific name of the corporation. Neath had long attained all except the last two and there now seemed little doubt that the borough was now fully incorporated. There was little else in it that was new. The charter specified the right to elect a Portreeve, twelve Aldermen and a Common Council of fifteen burgesses. A Common Clerk was, however, mentioned for the first time although this office was described as being held "as in times past." He was the keeper and recorder of the town's administrative records. No legal qualifications were required but he was expected to be an "honest and discreet" man!

Other offices to be elected were the Chamberlain or Common attorney, whose main duty was to collect all rents and dues belonging to the Council; two sergeants of the Mace who were to be responsible for carrying out the judgments of the court and to accompany the Portreeve and council on ceremonial occasions; the constables of the borough to keep the peace. Courts that were to be kept included a Court of Records held every fortnight and the ancient Court of Pie Powder to deal with matters pertaining to the three fairs and weekly market. The Court of Records was an all purpose court dealing with all manner of pleas, actions, suit and trespass and all offences against the statutes, liberties and dues of the borough involving sums up to £100. The office of Reve involved responsibility for executing court judgments. The obligation to serve was compulsory and unpaid and any burgess refusing office was liable to a fine of £5.

The Portreeve nominated was John Llewellyn (most probably of the Ynysygerwn estates). He was required, as were all other officers, to swear an oath of loyalty, before the Constable of the Castle, on taking office. It read as follows "You shall swear to serve our sovereign lord the King, the lord of this Borough and the Constable of the Castle whilst in the office of Portreeve until another be sworn in, to administer equal justice as well to the poor as the rich to the best of your cunning, wit and power. You shall diligently procure such things to be done as shall honestly and justly be to the profit of the said town of Neath and shall endeavour yourself to the utmost of your power to all heresies, treason, felonies and all trespasses and misdemeanours whatsoever committed within this borough during your term of office and the offender duly punished according to the law. You shall support the Common good of this town and faithfully behave yourself for the benefit, worship and credit of this town and its inhabitants. So help you God."

This oath along with others, was recorded by Pleydell Courteen (1705-1755), steward of the Gnoll estates and of the manor of Neath in a book which, eventually passed into the hands of James Coke, several times Portreeve of the town in the early eighteen hundred's.

The oath of the Recorder or Town Clerk was recorded as — "You shall swear to well and truly serve the Constable of the Castle, Portreeve, Aldermen and Burgesses of this town in the office of Recorder or Town Clerk and duly see all plaints, actions and processes in the courts holden before the Constable of the Castle or the Portreeve and records such as ought to be recorded, according to the custom of the Borough, taking for the same your due fees and fines. You shall truly write, extract yearly for the buying and gathering therefore. You shall not utter or disclose any secret of the said corporation and shall try, do and execute all that is appropriate to your office according to the best of your knowledge. So help you, God!" The oath demanded of the Aldermen was recorded in the following manners. "You shall swear you will truly serve our sovereign Lord the King, the Constable of the Castle, Portreeve and inhabitants as one of the Aldermen or Capital Burgesses and to endeavour that equal justice to the poor as well as the rich is administered to the best of your wit, cunning and power. You shall not utter or disclose any secret things or matter touching the fellowship or corporation of this town whereby any hindrance, prejudice or slander shall arise out of the same and shall honestly demean yourself with respect." The oath of the burgesses was in a similar vein.

This Jacobean Charter reinforced the character of a "close" corporation and did nothing to expand the obligations of the council to administer for the general good. Their functions were still mainly judicial and other responsibilities were exceedingly vague. There was little resemblance to any real system of local government. In fact, there is little evidence that the charter was really implemented. The truth of the matter was that two other bodies had been operating in the role of local government for a very lengthy period; namely, the Parish and the Quarter Sessions, both of these playing a very important part in the history of local administration. They were interwoven with the manorial borough as functioning bodies and to successfully disentangle them into a coherent picture would be an impossible task. But of the comparatve importance of the Manor, Borough, Parish and Quarter Sessions at the end of the seventeenth century so much is clear. The manor and the manorial courts were in an advanced stage of decay. The Borough was, inextrictably, bound up with the manorial courts and, with its "close" corporation character, showed signs of stagnation. The difficulty of dealing with the Parish and the Quarter Sessions have not survived before the early years of the eignteenth century. Before this, therefore, we can only speak in general terms as far as Neath is concerned.

The Parish

The Parish had always played an important part in the life of the community since the Middle Ages. Besides levying a rate for the maintenance of the Church, it had also accepted an obligation to alleviate the lot of the poor by organising almsgiving. By the time of the Tudors, pauperism had increased and the problem of poverty began to deeply concern the Elizabethan Parliaments. Not simply were there many poor people, but great numbers of these were without any means of sustenance whatever except what they could beg or were forced to steal. They formed a class of vagrants, which in some parts of the country, made up almost ten per cent of the population.

Apart from humanitarian considerations, it was felt that hordes of starving vagabonds constituted a threat to law and order. This concern expressed itself in several Acts for the relief of the poor which were consolidated in the great Elizabethan Poor Law Act of 1601. This was a piece of legislation so comprehensive that it remained almost intact until the Poor Law Amendment Act of 1834.

How did this mass pauperism come about? The closing of the monasteries and the secularisation of the medieval "hospitals" had, undoubtedly, helped in the process. Deprived of alms and other forms of help which the landless class had received from these sources, many turned to vagrancy seeking help where they could find it. But there were many other sources of mendicancy. Greedy landlords caused unemployment and homelessness by enclosure of common land and rackrenting. Then there were demobilised soldiers and sailors, many of them maimed, who received very little or no help from the state and were driven to begging in order to keep alive. Professional beggars male and female, were prominent in this class. Many of them had developed an expertise in pilfering and some of the girls and women relied on harlotry. Providing some colour to this otherwise melancholy scene, were the strolling players, singers and dancers. They generally "slept rough" but were, sometimes, fortunate to obtain a night's shelter and food in return for entertainment.

The Poor Law Act concerned itself with two classes of poor. One was the old and impotent. To deal with this problem the Parish was expected to levy a poor rate on all parishioners and appoint an officer (Overseer of the Poor) to execute it. From these funds (and from "poor boxes" placed in churches) payments were doled out to those who were incapable of any work. The other class comprised the able-bodied unemployed. The aim here was to set them to work which would yield a profit. Pauper children were apprenticed, as soon as they came of age, to the wealthier of the inhabitants. Raw materials, such as flax, hemp and wool were distributed to the unemployed who received fixed payments for the finished products. Any refusal or reluctance to work, meant a period in the House of Correction or a whipping or both. The Overseers were nominated by the Justices or, sometimes, directly by the church wardens. They were unpaid and were very often quite unsuitable for the office. A reluctance to serve was natural. Who would want to sacrifice time spent from his own job of making a living as a blacksmith or carpenter to take on an unpaid onerous office for which he had received no training? Inefficiency was inevitable and corruption always a possibility. To keep the poor rate down by discouraging pauperism was the dominant motive behind Poor Law administration. Vagrants on entering a parish and caught begging, found themselves at the whipping post and then sent on their way. Those who were able and willing to work were sometimes allowed to seek employment where they could find it, but anyone unable or unwilling to work was sent back to their own parish by a special settlement law. The impact which wandering vagrants made on entering a town is immortalised in the following nursery rhyme:

"Hark, hark! The dogs do bark
The beggars are coming to town,
Some gave them white bread and some gave them brown,
And some gave them a horse-whip and sent them out of town."

The brutality of officialdom was certainly tempered by the consciences of some individuals, as the rhyme suggests. The compassion found expression in the bequests which were sometimes in wills for the relief of the poor; an annual sum of £40 by Joan ap Leyson in 1634, £11. ten shillings by John Gibbs in 1670 (who also left an almshouse in Water Street for female paupers) were typical. There were many similar bequests made during the eighteenth century which will be referred to in later pages.

The first Parish vestry record for Neath which has survived, is dated July 1673, in which payments were detailed for maimed soldiers (demobolised after service in Ireland and on the Continent in wars against Spain). The two churchwardens were John Llewellyn, Portreeve and M. Jenkins. The presence of the Portreeve on the Vestry Committee is typical of the intermingling of functions and personnel in the various bodies concerned in local administration. In the following year, items for wines for the Church and further payments for maimed soldiers appear. In a vestry minute book of 1698, the following entries occur:

Paid for a horse to carry a cripple to the parish next and for meat and drink £6 and eight pence.
Order to remove three small children from the town four shillings and six pence.
For Wm Smith, a disbanded soldier, who had a pass from the Portreeve six pence.
To Wm Smith for supplying lodgings for maimed soldiers one shilling and six pence.

The rejection of a cripple and three small children and their removal to another parish is illustrative of the sheer inhumanity of aspects of the Poor Law in a practice.

The reference to a Portreeve's pass is an example of how a license to beg could be granted by the town authorities in certain cases; also recorded was s payment of one shilling and ten pence towards the upkeep of Cardiff Bridge and the House of Correction. This was a county rate which was exacted from the parish.

The other problem which concerned Parliament was the state of the roads. The Highway Act, passed in 1555, remained the foundation of highway lay for nearly three centuries. Constant references to the necessity of repairing roads in local records show that Neath shared in the appalling condition of roads everywhere. It was recorded in one parish that, although they risked their souls by refusing to attend Church, they were avoiding as great a risk to their bodies for, between the village and the church, "there were several Waters and the same Waters at manye tymes of the yeare due rise with the land fluds and the people cannot passe over the same without danger of drowning and cannot pass by the highwaye."

Under the Act, the surveyor appointed by the Parish Vestry (but after 1691, by the Justices) organised four days labout on the roads annually. Those who kept horses had to provide a cart and horse. The four days were extended to six days by later legislation. Like other duties, that of the

Surveyor was reluctantly undertaken but, if anyone refused, he was liable to a fine of £1 in 1555 and £5 in the 1691 legislation. His only consolation was that the term of office was for one year only to be relieved by an equally inexperienced and reluctant neighbour on a roat system. It was hardly surprising that no effective results ensued. In an effort to remedy the situation a highway rate was levied on the bases of an ordinance passed in 1654. The rate was not to exceed one shilling in the £. This lapsed at the Restoration and it was not until 1691, that a permanent highway rate was established.

By the end of the Stuart Period, the parish had become the most important local government in the country. It is estimated that parochial expenditure amounted to one fifth the national income. Yet no constitution had ever been given it nor had any legislation created it. Parish boundaries were fixed by local tradition. Periodically, a walk round the Parish boundaries was organised; in some places, it was the custom to beat, at intervals, the children taking part in the walk, so that they would always remember where the boundaries were! No definition existed of what constituted a parishioner but payment of rates could be demanded of any owner of a house or land whether resident or not. All parishioners could, in theory attent the Parish vestry but in Neath it was attended by a number of the prominent residents only, suggesting a Parish oligarchy.

The power of the Parish administration rested on the shoulders of the churchwardens. "Here in this country," wrote a contemporary observer, "with us, if a man's stock of a few beasts be his own, that he is out of debt, and pays his rent duly, we hold him a very rich and sufficient man — one that is able to render to the king and country good service. We make him a constable, a sidesman, at length, a church warden. Thus we raise him by degrees to the final honour. Here is the greatest governor among us." Toulmin Smith regarded chuch wardens as the very foundation of democratic local government and there is a great deal of validity in this view. Originally, the church warden was a church officer responsible for the church maintenance in all its aspects in consultation with the priest. Under the Tudors, he incurred many civil duties, as we have seen, in relation to the Poor and Highway laws. He became subordinate to the Justices but the actual work had to be carried out by him which was a formidable mixture of civil and secular duties. Perhaps one of the most difficult was the operation of the rescusancy laws which meant seeking out and fining those who did not attend church. It is easy to imagine the difficulties a conscientious warden would encounter with those of his neighbours who resented attending the Anglican Church. And what enormous tact he would require to arrange the new seatings in the Church! The job of supervising the duties of other church officers would be his —

the Parish Cleri, Sexton and, in some parishes especially in Wales, the Dog Whipper. The latter's duty was to preserve order amongst the dogs who accompanied their owners to church and also to drive out animals which could not be controlled. Wooden tongs were used for gripping the offenders by the neck. A pair is preserved at Clodock in Herefordshire.

Many of the secular offices of the Parish were excused for money payments by those who could afford it, which was manifestly unjust to those who could not. But the duties were so onerous that there were no religious tests like those which applied to corporation officials. Neither were there any property qualifications.

The Quarter Sessions

Mention must be made of the other body of local government, the Court of Quarter Sessions and the Justices who operated it. Despite the dominance of the Parish, at the end of the seventeenth century it was already showing signs of a more lasting quality. Indeed, the growing subordination of Parish officers to the local Justices of the Peace, was a check on the autonomy of the Parish.

The Quarter Sessions Court was a product of the Act of Union and the desire of the Tudors to end lawlessness in Wales; and to bring the country in line with England where Justices who assembled in the Quarter Sessions and were assigned to keep the peace and administer justice generally. Besides judicial business, which continued up until 1972, the justices were concerned with certain matters of civil administration. Simple at first, this grew during the centuries as the population increased and towns developed. The absence of records for Neath (and Glamorgan generally) up to the early years of the eighteenth century, is extremely frustrating but, at least, we have records of the operation of this court in one place in Wales, namely Caernarfon. This covers a period from 1541 to 1558, which gives a clear idea of how this court carried out its business during the first years of its life.

The chief offences dealt with were assaults, riotous assemblies and forcible entries. Such behaviour was almost a way of life at that time. Welshmen were by nature quicktempered and ready to take offence and the social and economic conditions provided a source of endless grievances. Enclosures, rack-renting and evictions were creating a landless class and dissension was easily bred.

The usual sentences for assaults were fines and a binding over to keep the peace by a complicated system of the taking out of recognisances for ensuring future good behaviour. Punishments for petty theft were, however, savagely brutal. It was evident that offences against property were regarded as far more serious than against people, an attitude which was to persist up to our own times. Cases were recorded of the hands being branded for petty theft. Other punishments were flogging and a period in the stocks or pillory. Many cases of women offenders were recorded. These were punished with the same brutality as men. One case appears of a woman found guilty of stealing a loaf of bread and cheeses worth six pence. She was sentenced to be flogged both in Caernarvon and in her own neighbouring town. Even more savagely brutal was the sentence on "Margaret ferch Ieuan ap Madog of the Ffestiniog" who stole a cheese worth one penny and a sixpenny coin. She was ordered to be flogged and then nailed by the ear to the pillory in the market place. All these were described as having no lands or goods of any kind and it was noticeable that those of a higher social status were subject to fines only for similar offences. The attitude to the starving vagrant was that, if he or she were ferociously punished for the "crime" of poverty, this social problem would disappear. It never did, of course, and it was the recognition of this fact that, eventually, led to the Elizabethan Poor Law legislation to deal with such poverty. The reference to the theft of cheese is a reminder of the practice in parts of North Wales, for a husband and wife, who had little or no possessions, to go begging during the first year of their marriage. Each went their separate ways. The husband would travel the shires begging for grain and other seeds during the harvest whilst the wife wandered through the countryside begging for cheese, wool and flax. These women were known as "Gwragedd Cawsa" or cheese gatherers. The court, also, dealt with offences against trading regulations, faulty weights and measures and the unlawful plwying of cards and dice.

The Welsh gentry, who were already establishing themselves before the Act of Union, welcomed the setting up of the Quarter Sessions and readily donned the mantle of the Justic of the Peace. Acting singly or in pairs, or through the sessions court, they became, eventually, the real administrators of the county. Of the actual effect of the Act of Union on law and order in Wales, there was somewhat of a disparity of opinion. At one end of the scale is Burke's opinion.

> "From that moment," he wrote, "as by a charm, tumults subsided. Obedience was restored and civilisation followed in the train of liberty. The day star of the English Constitution had arisen in their hearts and all was harmony within and without."

This view was, of course, so much nonsense. Many members of the South Wales gentry, the Mansels, Tubervilles and Carnes, were corrupt and bellicose in their behaviour. They continued to employ small bands of retainers (as in pre-Tudor times) who were often little more than hired thugs. These they used to commit acts of robbery and violence. Another problem were juries who refused to convict, and there was always the difficulty of catching offenders and bringing them to Court. Although Welsh was forbidden by law to be used in the courts, in actual practice it was found impracticable to operate in a largely monoglot coutry; Welsh was, therefore, permitted in court when necessary and interpreters allowed. There was more justice in courts from that angle in later centuries in Wales, but English remained the official language, and this contributed in no small way to the anglicisation of the Welsh gentry. Whether English Laws benefitted Wales from the point of view of law and order the truth must lie between the roseate view of Burke and the severe criticism which can easily be levelled on conditions which prevailed in Wales in the Sixteenth century. Compared with the chaotic conditions of the fifteenth century, a new legal system and the destruction of the feudal power of the Marcher lords can only be described as an improvement.

At the end of the Stuart Period, it was very obvious that there was little semblance of any organised system of local administration and the attempt, in these pages, to draw together the various strands of local governmental activities into some pattern, can hardly claim to have succeeded. The truth was that civic consciousness had not yet developed sufficiently to embrace the idea of what local government should be, which was a regard for the full social, economic and cultural needs of the community. Until that happened, the hotch-potch of local government bodies was bound to continue. But from the economic side, Neath, at the end of the seventeenth century, was in reasonable shape and was described by the Webbs as a thriving little town. It had recovered from the temporary recession in the coal trade due to the efforts of Sir Humphrey Mackworth and it became, with Swansea, the leading exporter of coal in the county. The iron industry was also beginning to develop and the copper industry had grown into an activity which made Neath the chief centre for the production of refined copper in the county. The market and fair activities supplied another economic buttress. Neath, unlike many other Welsh boroughs, had the economic resources to survive and develop although the reason for its existence as a garrison town had long disappeared. In physical terms, it had developed little from early Tudor times, except for an area North and West of the castle, with a population of about 1000.

Six centuries had passed since Richard de Granville had set up the garrison which became the borough of Neath. The space of growth had been extremely slow but the Industrial Revolution was to come, bringing with it rapid and far-reaching social and economic changes which, in turn, were to have profound effects on local administration.

CHAPTER 7

Neath under the Hanoverians

How much should Parliament interfere in local government? This is a perennial problem and the final answer has yet to be made. Under the Stuart Kings, Charles II and James II, there was, as we have seen, the most flagrant interference but successive Parliaments in the eighteenth century, under the Hanoverian Georges, took an exactly opposite view. To them the state should not be bothered with local affairs but should concentrate on national and international problems.

In theory, therefore, the period 1688 to the Municipal Reform Act of 1835, with which we are now concerned, should have been a period of unrestricted Municipal growth; but, in actual fact, Neath Borough was subjected to a domination of a family which completely stultified its development. It was the age of the Mackworths.

In the previous century the Constable of the Castle, the lord's representative, became an increasingly shadowy figure whilst the Portreeve (broadly speaking the people's man) became the real head of the manorial courts. The Leet, the people's court, tended to overshadow the Court Baron in which the Constable of the Castle was dominant. But now all was to change and Neath borough fell completely under the control of the Mackworths despite several attempts on the part of a section of the burgesses to resist this power. It is to this family we must now turn to examine the part it played in the history of local government in Neath.

The first of the family was Sir Humphrey Mackworth (1657-1724) who, although a qualified barrister with an assured professional career in London, settled down in Neath having married, in 1686, Mary Evans, the heiress to the Gnoll Estates. The marriage excited much critical comment regarding Sir Humphrey's motives. This is reflected in the following lines written by a local writer of lampoons.

"Sir Humphrey has got the art
To make his lady part
With a good old ancient estate.

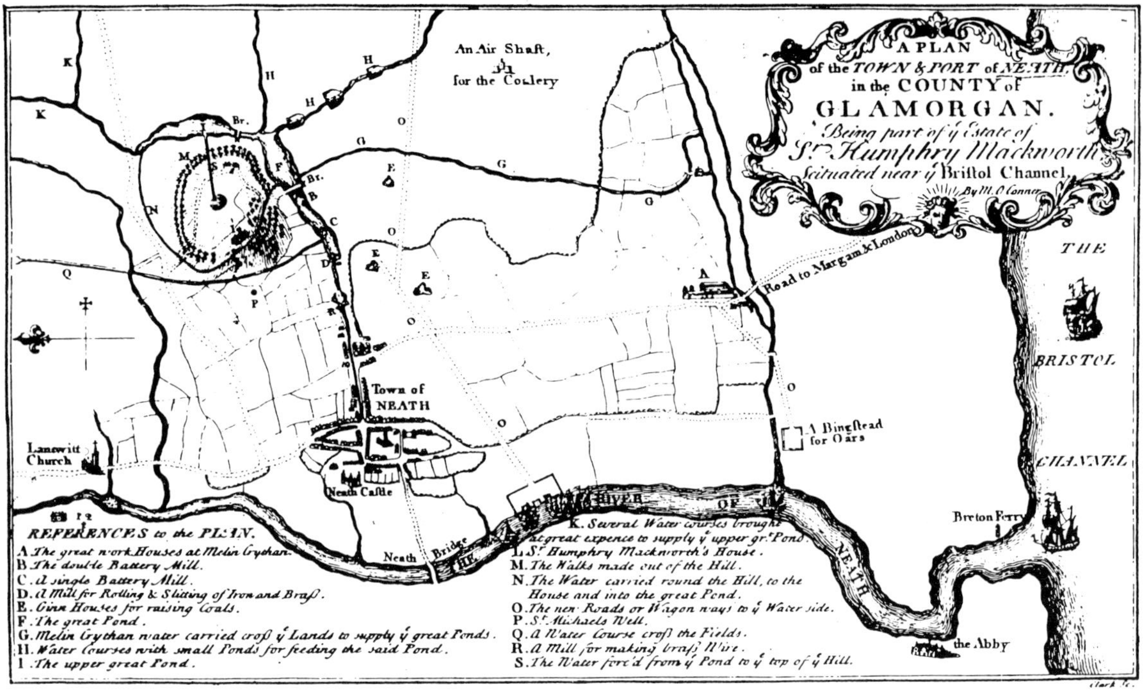

M. O'Conner's Plan of Neath, 1720.
(By permission of the British Museum).

He applauds for a wit
She may silently sit
To repent when it is all too late!"

Whether or not this view was justified can hardly be known but the marriage certainly fitted into Mackworth's declared ambitions to become rich and powerful. Yet this was only one side of one of the most fascinating, complex characters it is possile to imagine. He proved to be an enterprising and imaginative but unscrupulous industrialist, a man of pronounced religiosity but a local administrator of almost "Tammany Hall" proportions. Sir Humphrey had rescued the coal industry from a period of depression to a flourishing concern by 1690. By 1713, he had established the manufacture of copper, brass, lead and silver refined from lead.

But it was through the coal industry that he became involved deeply in local administrative affairs. The burgesses had long enjoyed valuable trading rights relating to coal (one of the many exclusive commercial privileges they had clung to for so long).

Sir Humphrey's wife's family, the Evans' of the Gnoll had held coal leases with the corporation for many years and the burgesses were allowed cheap coal (two pence per barrow) and were also paid one shilling for every "wey" of coal exported. The leases were due for renewal in 1697 and, because Mackworth was using much of the coal for his copper smelting at Melyn-Crythan, the burgesses were gaining little from the small exports. So they refused to renew the leases. The stage was set for Sir Humphrey to move and attempt to establish a control of the council. This would ensure the renewal of his leases and satisfy his social and political ambitions. He was already Constable of the Castle and he used this position to infiltrate into the council by appointing burgesses of his own choosing. One of these was Thomas Jenkins, Mackworth's own agent. An agreement was eventually patched up but his appetite for power had been whetted and he now planned to dominate the town's courts. Mackworth decided to work through his steward Philip Williams. The latter bought up houses and claimed burgesses rights based upon them. He set up standings in the street to break the power of the burgesses who had always controlled these. Obstructions were placed on the operation of the Court Leet and, from then on, the Court Baron began to establish supremacy with the Constable of the Castle replacing the Portreeve as "Mayor" of the borough.

The traditional method of all petty dictators to further their power was adopted and tenants of small holdings were threatened with eviction unless they supported Mackworth. The independence of the burgesses was further threatened by the election of John Davies, Mackworth's agent, as Portreeve. Resistance from some of the burgesses persisted and, when an attempt was made by Mackworth to elect officers, a drama of "Clochmerle" character was enacted. The burgesses proceeded from the Church to the Town Hall to elect officers. Mackworth and his supporters kept watch on them and, as soon as they were clear of the church, rushed up to the church porch and there declared the appointments of the town officers. But, by this time, the burgesses' party came charging back to the church. On their approach, Mackworth and his gang withdrew and hastily made their way back to his residence.

Sometime early in 1704, serious quarrelling broke out between Thomas Mansel and Sir Humphrey over the coal trade. Mansel feared competition and its effects on his collieries at Briton Ferry and Swansea. He was determined to disrupt the export of coal from the Mackworth mines. There was strong feeling against Sir Humphrey resulting from his policy of employing immigrant workers from Shropshire. These people were accused by the Neath Burgesses of loose living and all kinds of debaucheries as well as causing local unemployment. They turned to the Mansels for help. Sir Thomas Mansel of Margam and his fellow justices arranged for the forcible impressment of a number of miners and the rumour was spread, deliberately, that this was the fore-runner of the impressing of more than 200 men. The justifiable terror which men regarded service in the army or navy of those days expressed itself in a wholesale evacuation of the works. Everyone fled, and hid themselves in the woods or wherever they could.

Both Mackworth and the Mansels claimed they were serving the interests of the burgesses. The former took the view that he had brought prosperity and much employment to the town. His philosophy was, to paraphrase an American business dictum, "what was good for Mackworth was good for the town." The Mansels claimed that they were protecting the burgesses against the autocracy of Mackworth. In 1706, both Mansels died. This was described by Mackworth as "a deliverance from fire!" But serious trouble was in store for him. An enquiry was held into conditions of the lead and copper mines in Cardigan owned by the Mine Adventurers. Mackworth came out badly. The company, which had copper works in Cardigan as well as in Neath, was forced into bankruptcy in 1709, and Mackworth, as chief shareholder and Deputy Governor of the company, was arraigned before the bar of the Commons. He was found "guilty of many and notorious frauds" but the coalition government collapsed and the Tories obtained power, which resulted in the Bill against Mackworth (a Tory) being dropped. However, he was dismissed from the Company although, in 1713, his resilience was demonstrated by the setting up of another Company (the Mineral Manufacturers) although this again ran into trouble. But the final assessment of Mackworth as pioneer industrialist in Neath must surely be a favourable one. He had given the town a major industrial boost in the early days of the Industrial Revolution and the fertility of his ideas found expression in the ingenious system of tramways, and waterways which made Neath into a veritable inland port. One of his most original ideas of transport was that of sailing waggons. By the attachment of sails it was calculated that, when there was a breeze, one horse could do the work of twenty.

However, it was his involvement in local politics which must be our real concern and, in the relationship between Mackworth and the burgesses, a compromise was eventually reached in which the privileges of the latter would be protected provided that they, in turn, would accept and acknowledge the political dominance of this extraordinary man; and he certainly was of a "larger than life" dimension. His great abilities were, as we have seen, marred by his lack of scruple. He was inordinately ambitious. "Tis plain that Sir Humphrey Mackworth aims at nothing less than universal monarchy in Glamorgan" wrote one William Phillips to Sir Edward Mansel. He lived, certainly, beyone his means although the magnificence of his house in the Gnoll added dignity and splendour to the town. In his diary which fills four note books, now in the keeping of the Neath Antiquarian Society, he constantly expressed pious thoughts about events and people and exhibited a sense of guilt which would have done credit to a seventeenth century Puritan. The Mackworth file contains many of the religous and political tracts which he wrote. One was entitled, "The Divine Authority of the Scriptures", another was described as "A Bill for better relief and settlement of the Poor". Mackworth had a great interest in political and constitutional subjects and a typical tract was entitled, "A Free Parliament or a Vindication of the Commons Assembled". He was a founder member of the Society for the Promotion of Christian Knowledge in 1699 and it was he who persuaded the Society to extend their interest to Wales. A charity work school was established for the children of his employees in the Melyn. Sir Humphrey ceased subscribing to this school in 1703 owing to troubles with the corporation. This then was the dominant personality in Neath in the eighteenth century, and one of the most remarkable in its history. Such was the astonishing complexity of his character that each quality was matched by a direct contradiction. He was only too well aware of his faults and was always extremely remorseful concerning them; yet he did nothing about it. He was always a lavish host and on one occasion he stated in his diary — "Upon the arrival of some Vessells, I thought it was in my Interest to treate the Masters of ye Coal vessells which I did with punch which Inspired us to Excess. I committed a great sin therein; I am heartily sorry for it; God forgive me, for Jesus Christ sake." But he never became sober in his habits and, generally, lived extravagantly to the end of his life yet never ceasing to express penitence.

After his death, in 1727, he was succeeded by his son, Herbert who occupied many high offices including that of High Sheriff and M.P. for Glamorgan Boroughs. The family tradition was carried on by his son, Sir Herbert Mackworth, who succeeded to the estates in 1765 serving as M.P. until his death in 1791 at the age of 54 from a poisoned finger. He was a very dominant personality but possessed many attractive qualities. His death caused great distress to his wife and family. He left £60,000 and an estate worth £5,000 a year.

The last of the Mackworth family was Sir Robert Humphrey Mackworth. He married Molly, daughter of Nathaniel Miers of Cadoxton Lodge. She was sixteen at the time and, according to contemporary reports, extremely beautiful. Sir Robert died in 1794 and bequeathed Gnoll House and all his property to his wife who remarried in 1797. Her second husband was Capel Hanbury Leigh.

Each member of the Mackworth family, following the first Sir Humphrey, had played a dominant role in the political life of the borough. In the period 1760-1780, the first during which consistent corporation records existed, we find that no less than five members of the ruling family sat as Aldermen, together with a non-resident Mackworth

Sir Herbert Macworth 1st Bart. by Dean after Russell.
(By permission of the National Museum of Wales).

nominee who lived in London. Making up the rest of the Aldermanic bench, were two tenants of the Mackworth family, William Cross, manager of the local collieries, and Sir Noah Thomas, physician to King George III. The office of Portreeve was held by William Cross on five occasions. This was typical of a system by which the Mackworths themselves allowed their puppets to carry on the day to day administration of the borough. There was, of course the Parliamentary representation of the borough. This was their chief value in the eighteenth century and the Mackworths enjoyed fifty one unbroken years of such power. They represented the new aristocracy of wealth which had come to rival the old aristocracy of birth, in social and political power.

The Quarter Sessions

In dealing with this court and the work of Justices in the eighteenth century, our task is immeasurably easier than in previous centuries because Glamorgan session records are available. In these it is evident that the administrative work which the courts had gradually taken on had grown considerably as the town developed. Various indictable offences, matters relating to Poor Law relief, the maintenance of highways and bridges, supervision of Parish administration had all become the responsibility of the Quarter Sessions. Some of the work delegated to Petty Sessional Courts, or special courts such as the Brewster Sessions and Badger Courts for itinerant pedlars. There was also the licensing of Protestant Dissenters' meetings and theatrical performances; with increasing legislation, the work of the Sessions grew accordingly. At times, they sat almost continuously, instead of four times a year as normal.

A typical day in Court is recorded in 1760 when the Quarter Sessions met in Neath. The Keeper of the Rolls, the Earl of Plymouth, had signed a Precept commanding the Sheriff of Glamorgan (William Currie) to summon before the Justices at the next Quarter Sessions to be held at Neath on 15th July, 1766, all coroners, stewards of great men, bailiffs, portreeves and chief constables. The Precept, also signed by the Clerk of the Peace, was ordered to be displayed in all public places. At the sessions, the sheriff presented his Sacrament Certificate proving he had taken Holy Communion in the Parish Church of Wick and that he conformed to the tenets of the Church of England. This Certificate was witnessed by the clergyman and the church wardens. By the Test Act of 1662, this certificate was necessary to prove that all office holders were not Roman Catholics or Non-conformists. They were debarred from office. There was also an oath book containing the Oath of Abjuration declaring King George the rightful King and abjuring the claims of the Pretender. This, also, had to be subscribed by office holders. All the business of the court was entered in a minute book by the Clerk of the Court.

The most common offences recorded related to an assault and the theft of the daily necessities of living, food and clothes. There was one indictment against workers who attempted to unite for higher wages than the miserable rates which were paid them. Eleven men from Neath "being workmen and labourers in the art, mystery and manual occupation of a Collier and not being content with work at the usual rate, did unlawfully assemble and meet together and conspire and agree that none would work for a lesser rate than 'Nine Score Fathom for four shillings and one penny', when the accustomed price was three shillings and five pence." No sentence was recorded. It would have been illuminating, if it had. As in the Caernavon Calendar, trivial sentences were passed on offenders guilty of violent assault. People were not sacrosanct in the way property was. This attitude was as deeply entrenched as ever. Assaults were subject to a fine or a recognisance to appear at the next court. But thefts, however, were punished with barbarous severity. The stealing of two silk handkerchiefs and a ribbon brought a sentence of transportation to Africa for seven years with little hope of return. The expenses recorded for taking a defendant from Cardiff to London in chains, and thence on to the convict hulk for transportation to Africa was £17 thirteen shillings and four pence. This sum was far in excess of the goods stolen. In addition, there was a sum five guineas for the cost of the passage to Africa. A case of fraud, of a somewhat humorous character, was recorded in respect of a defendant named William Herbert of Cadoxton. He was charged with "fraudulently and deceitfully fixing on the head of a certain yellow ox (worth thirty shillings) the horns of another beast and fraudulently sell the same ox to Richard Jenkins, for the sum of £4 to the great damage and deceit of Richard Jenkins." The defendant was fined six pence. Expenses claimed by a gaoler tell us more of the penal code and its operation at that time.

Paid for the expense of whipping a felon for stealing wheat = £1.0.0.
To expenses for executing Francis Rosser for murder.
Paid Hangman = £4.0.0.
Paid for horse and cart to hale him to the gallows = £1.0.0.
Paid for halter = £0.0.6.
Paid for horses and cart to bring his body to Neath to be hung in chains = £4.0.0.

A macabre curiosity might prompt the question as to where in Neath the body was hanged. Tradition points to Warren Hill, in Briton Ferry.

The variety of cases recorded is illustrated by the conviction of John

Rendall, master of the sloop. "The Love and Unity" for casting a large amount of ballast into the River Neath. He was fined thirty shillings, half of which went to the poor of Neath. In 1777, William Williams, a Neath victualler, was indicted for keeping ten hogs near a dwelling "where he doth feed them with offal of beasts and other filth." In earlier years, this would have come before the Court Leet.

In 1698, a case was recorded of William Morgan of Neath, gent, "being an impious profane and irreligious person and not having the fear of God in his heart but moved and seduced by the instigation of the devil and intending to vilify the true Christian religion, said in Neath on December 31st, these false impious and blasphemous words:

> *'This world was not made by God but was made before there was a God; nor do I believe in the Holy Scriptures and Moses was either a fool or a liar and he made the scriptures to be but a fable to the grievous scandal of the true religion . . .' In contempt of our said, Lord the King and his laws." In the spring of 1800, John Griffiths of Neath, a labourer, was convicted of saying, "Damn King George III, I'll make a better King than him out of an orl tree only gilding and painting it and sending it to Parliament." He was imprisoned for two months and bound in recognisances.*

The Vagrancy Acts of 1530, 1698 and 1702 and the operation of the Poor Law Act of 1601, dealt harshly with vagrants. Much of the work which the Parish Vestry carried out seem to have now devolved upon the Quarter Session Courts. Throughout the eighteenth century, cases were recorded relating to the relief of paupers and to the Act of Settlement whereby the poor were chargeable only to the parish of their origin. This legality could be achieved by a birth qualification, by serving as a Parish officer, by residing in a Parish for one year or by being apprenticed for seven years to a trade. Examples of vagrants being passed from parish to parish, the repair of highways and bridges, in which the Parish Surveyor was involved, occur in the Session records. A very confused picture of the working of the Sessions and Parish emerges. The power of levying rates, apparently, belonged to both bodies but the Quarter Sessions were taking up responsibility for payments for a variety of matters such as expenses for viewing ten bodies of men suffocated in the Wernfaith Colliery (in the Neath district) and a Bill for £6.0.0. presented by the Sheriff for organising festivities relating to a general thanksgiving for the end of the Seven Years War. The court issued pardons for the soldiers who had been in custody for desertion.

Other duties of the court included the compiling of Land Tax assessments under the 1780 Act. No one could vote unless his name appeared on the land tax list. A tax was raised on lights and windows by the Act of 1696. The tax was imposed on occupiers not landlords. Levies of six shillings were made for ten to twenty windows, ten shillings for twenty to thirty windows and thirty shillings for more than thirty. This explains bricked-up windows in many old houses. Another tax was levied on houses, carriages, horses and servants. An assessment in 1790 exists for Neath Genol hamlet (Cadoxton, Neath). Prices of corn sold in Neath and Cowbridge were recorded and the Clerk of the Peace had to inspect plans of canals, docks, railways and harbours before a Bill came up before the House.

The Toleration Act of 1688 allowed Protestant Dissenters to hold meetings, provided their meeting places and preachers were registered with the Quarter Sessions. Roman Catholics were not included in a Toleration Act until 1791. This was a time of the Revolution in France and the English Government, in sheer fright, passed a number of repressive laws such as the Unlawful Societies Act. Free masons were exempted from its penalties provided they returned a list of members to the Quarter Sessions. Under this Act, printing presses had to be registered with the Sessional Courts. In fact, these courts dealt with almost every aspect of civil as well as judicial administration (except for major indictable offences which were referred to the Great Sessions).

The practice of farming out contracts was beginning to be a feature of the late eighteenth century and one of the most scandalous examples of this policy related to prisons and Houses of Correction. In the early days of the century, gaolers were not paid but were allowed to extract what renumeration they could from the prisoners in return for food and the other necessities. It is easy to imagine the miserable plight of poor prisoners who could not afford to pay anything. In the latter part of the century, the gaoler is recorded as receiving a salary but a very small one. One gaoler complained that his net annual salary after paying a turnkey, was only £54, a factor which was bound to react in favour of the better off prisoners who could buy many privileges and to the detriment of the pauper class.

The House of Correction was intended for vagrants but was, later, used for the punishment of minor offences. The old Glamorgan House of Correction was in Cowbridge. A large stone was fixed over the central arch with a representation of the irons worn by prisoners. In 1829, it was closed and a new one opened in Swansea.

The Parish

The parish, in the era up to 1835, was on the decline although it persisted in Neath long after the Poor Law Amendment Act of 1834 which was assumed to have killed it off. At the end of the eighteenth century, complaints began to mount up concerning the rates which had to be levied for poor relief and which was usually in the region of three shillings in the pound. In a Vestry minute book of 1798, the overseer was cautioned about the amount of relief granted and was ordered to discontinue certain payments. The parish now, referred many items to the Justices.

The eighteenth century parish records indicate a wide variety of business enacted at Vestry meeting despite its declining importance and subordination to the Quarter Sessions. The granting of relief to the needy in money and in kind was a recurring item throughout the century. But such orders had to be signed by the Justices. A typical case was a grant of eight shillings each to Lawrence Bailey and Beryl Griffiths for house rent and general needs. The orders were signed by two Justices. It was one of the duties of the Vestry to issue registered pauper lists and make additions or deletions as they saw fit. Vermin control had always been, and continued to be, a parish obligation. The hedgehog seemed to have been the chief target for there were numerous items of payments for such killings. For example, four hedgehogs would mean a payment of one shilling and four pence. Foxes were also, of course, looked upon as vermin and each fox would bring six pence to the killer upon the head being shown to the warden or overseer.

It was at the Vestry that the curfew ringer was paid (£1 per annum). The ringing of the curfew bell was originally for the purpose of warning people to cover up their fires for the night (wooden houses with thatched roofs were obviously, highly vulnerable to fire). It was also useful for giving the time. In Elizabethan times ale-house keepers had to close their premises at curfew. Later on, curfew ringing took on a religious significance and served to remind people of the necessity of repeating "Ave Maria". It was Alderman Davies, the early eighteenth century Portreeve and public benefactor, who was responsible for perpetuating the custom in Neath. In his will, he left £10 to the church wardens for the ringing of the 8 o'clock curfew.

It was the Parish which levied the poor rate, the church rate and highway rate (in later days, at the instructions of the Highway Board). In 1808, the poor rate was three shillings in the pound and the Overseer was warned to be more cautious about giving relief, to stop certain reliefs and to apply to the Justices to issue summons against rate defaulters whose number were increasing. The apprenticing of pauper children was an obligation of the wardens. In December 1808, a girl, Eliza Baker was apprenticed to one David Jones and we find that two quantities of cloth be given her. There were occasions when the vestry authority preferred to get rid of a problem even if it cost them money. The sum of £3 was given to one James Gordon to enable him to travel to London to seek employment "rather than that he should trouble this parish any longer". In a vestry meeting in January 1811, consideration was given to the building of a work house for the employment of the poor in order to relive the poor rate. It was decided to approach the new owner of the Gnoll Estate, Henry Grant to see if he had made up his mind about helping to set up a workhouse. It was also decided to ask him to arrange for paupers to be employed at the Melyn-Cryddan quarries. In many cases paupers were asked to carry out unpleasant jobs of such as the clearing out of sewers. After completing this job, they would be transferred to the quarries to cut stones for road repairs.

Council Administration

The passing of the Mackworths from the scene at the end of the century meant the end of a classic example of a family domination over a town. Neath had been a "pocket borough" par excellence. The Gnoll estates had now become part of the Monmouth estates of Capel Hanbury Leigh of Pontypool Park. The Gnoll House became vacant and remained so until 1811 when Grant took over. But during this interim period, a Mr George Johnstone began negotiations for its purchase and, between 1801 and 1808, was described as lord of the manor in the Court Leet and View of Frankpledge. But the final contract was never signed and legal difficulties resulted in the estates reverting to Leigh in 1808, until 1811 when they were sold to Henry Grant for £100,000.

By this time the Gnoll collieries had closed and cheap coal for the burgesses came to an end, although rent was still paid for the Corporation leases. As far as town government was concerned there was a significant change regarding the Constable of the Castle. Under the Mackworths, the Constable was always their nominee. During the absenteeism of Leigh, the corporation became temporarily in charge of their own affairs. William Gwyn, the Constable of the Castle became more of a town Clerk working with the council. The personnel of the Aldermanic bench included business and professional men instead of the lord's nominees. There were Thomas Leyshon, customs officer, W. Gronow, Surgeon; John King, ironmonger; John Morgan, shopkeeper. Together with four older members (Daniel Benbow, tallow chandler; Rees Rees, grocer; Thomas Edwards, draper and Richard Pendrill, shopkeeper and agent), a senior ruling group of nine emerged by 1805. It was now decided to increase the Aldermanic bench to twelve and to elect a Common Council of fifteen. This had been laid down in the Jacobean Charter which had never been fully implemented. The Common Council was to us now made up of ten resident tradesmen and others. The five remaining were Capel Leigh,

"Rheola", Neath, from south side of river by Thomas Horner.
(By permission of the National Museum of Wales).

himself (who would, naturally, be a non-participant) Nathaniel Miers, his brother-in-law, John Place, manager of the Mines Royal in Neath Abbey, his brother Thomas Place and a prominent solicitor in the town, James Coke, who was to occupy the office of Portreeve on four occasions. Disputes over the legality of the elections necessitated Counsel's opinion but the matter was settled to the satisfaction of the Council, and they remained in this form until 1827.

But what of the local courts? The Court Leet had virtually disappeared and the business of the Court Baron had largely been taken over by the monthly Court of Pleas. The Court of Pie Powder also sat intermittently. But little business in any court was done beyond the election of officers and an occasional civil action relating to leases and mortgages. There was little or none corporate activity. However, in 1811, the sale of the Gnoll estates to a Pembrokeshire gentleman, Henry Grant (his father was Rector of Roach) brought a new dominant personality to the scene and local government was given a certain directive force. Henry Grant was 68 at the time and it was his eldest son, Henry John Grant, who became involved in local politics. In less than two years, he was elected Portreeve in 1814 after serving as a Common Councillor and Alderman. However, the Mackworth-style domination returned for William Gwyn was dismissed by Grand and David Powell, a local solicitor and a steward of the Gnoll

Estate, took his place in an office which combined that of Constable of the Castle and Town Clerk. Soon Grant's nominees began to fill the Aldermanic bench and burgesses were gradually debarred from all participation in the town's affairs. But, unlike under the Machworths, some attempt was made to administer to the needs of the community. David Powell, who was now in a position of great power, made it known that the irresponsible practice of distributing to the burgesses any surplus corporate funds after expenses had been paid for, would cease. He instituted a close scrutiny of the finances of the borough and declared that any money saved would be spent on improvements in the town. Improvements in some of the main streets such as Wind Street, New Street and Church Place were made. Improving leases were issued and, 1819, it was resolved to obtain subscribers for a new Town Hall, not only for functional purposes, but also for aesthetic values.

The New Town Hall

At a meeting of the council on February 19, 1819 with the Portreeve, James Coke, in the chair, the feeling was general that the old Guildhall, in what is today called Old Market Street, was inadequate for public business and that a building of suitable dimension and character befitting the town should be built. It was decided to allocate £1,000 of corporation funds towards the cost and than an appeal be made to prominent people in the town and county for donations; such monies were to be deposited in the bank of Eaton and Gronow. The Corporation minutes of a March meeting record a decision to demolish an old building called "the old Dark House" to prepare for a site. Two months later, a contract was signed with W. Bowen, builders, of Swansea and, a year later, a contract with Mr Pliner to colour and paint the Hall and Market House (i.e. the Corn Market which was to occupy the ground floor). On June 22nd 1820, the foundation stone was laid with full masonic ceremony. The Brethren of the Beaufort lodge and Portreeve left the White Hart to meet the Burgesses at the site; after the ceremony they retired to the "Ship and Castle" for a celebration dinner. In terms of money, the new hall was to cost £2,250 with addition of £70 for the arcade and jury rooms. W. Whittington, was allowed the materials of the old hall for the sum of £50, this sum to be deducted from the extra £265 credited to him for "doing the interior of the hall." Fluted iron pillars graced the colonade. A description of the new hall in Lewis' Topographical Dictionary (1843) conveyed a contemporary impression of its appearance as a "neat commodious edifice in the Grecian style of architecture with the handsome receeding portico of the Ionic order but, being out of the line of the principal thoroughfare, it is not seen

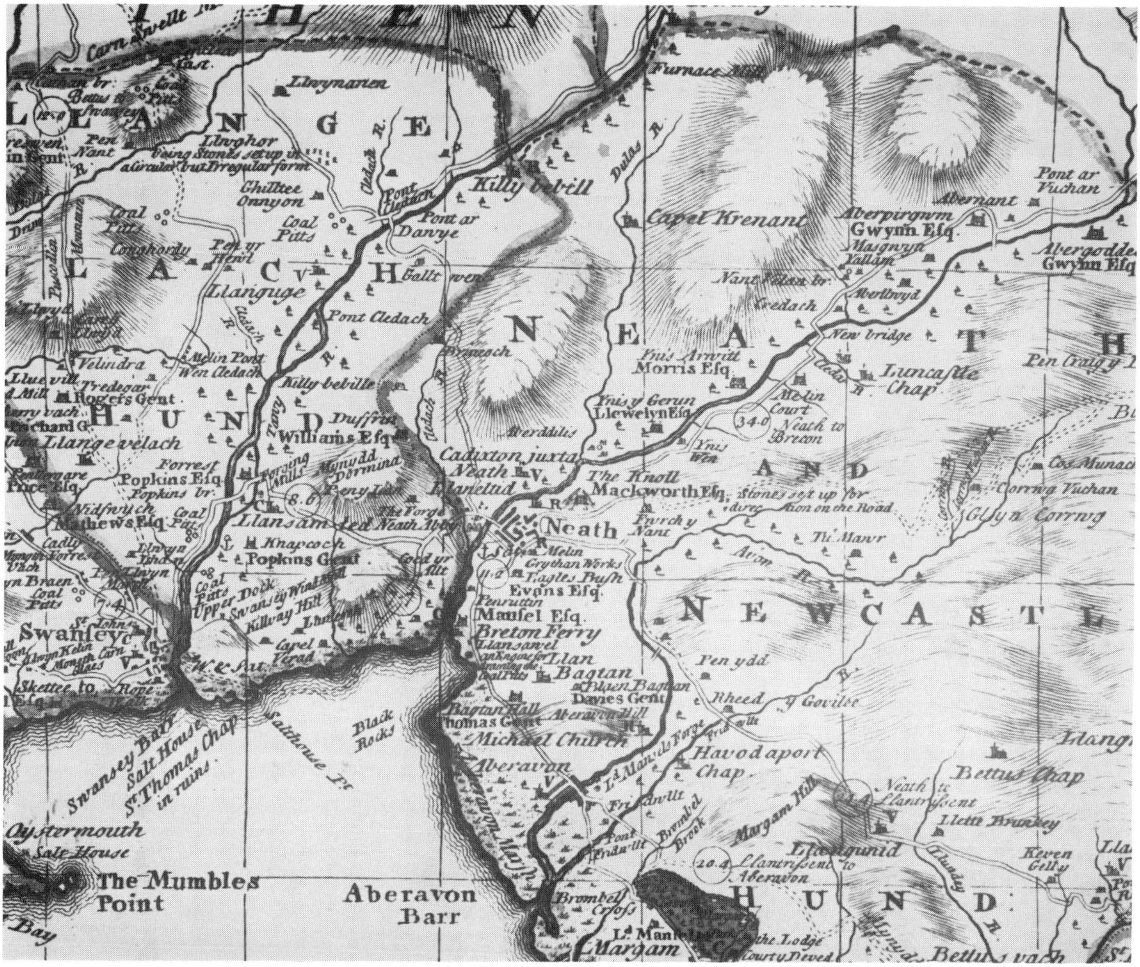

Part of Thomas Kitchin's Map of Glamorgan, 1754, showing Swansea and Neath.

to advantage. The upper part of the building contains a spacious Council Chamber with a jury room, and apartment for petty sessions and other business of the local Magistracy, and the lower part is appropriated for the use of the Corn Market." A public reading room was opened later, and in the "Handbook of the Vale of Neath", published in 1852, it was stated that one room was exclusively devoted to the purposes of a news room where the "Times" and the "Daily News" could be seen at four o'clock on the day of publication together with the principal Daily, Evening and Weekly papers, Metropolitan and Provincial. At first, the lower part was used for other produce as well as corn but, after the market was built in 1837, it was used only for the sale of corn. It continued to be used as such up to the end of the century when it was converted to a weighbridge and, later, a fire station. Two lock-up cells which were accommodated there, can still be seen today.

Later, in 1834, the idea of a new market was mooted. Interest was extended to other commercial matters and it was decided to set up a body of harbour trustees to improve facilities in the port of Neath.

But the demand for municipal reform was mounting, for local government throughout the county was but a travesty of what it should be. Many voluntary organisations were formed in these pre-reform days to meet the social demands which the Industrial Revolution had brought about. The Parish Constables, for instance, were quite unable to meet the demands made on them by increasing crime so the local inhabitants took matters into their own hands and set up an "Association for Prosecution of Felons" in 1813. This operated almost up to the 1835 Municipal Reform Act. The usual method of operation was to issue advertisements offering rewards above the scale allowed by law; for burglary and highway robbery the reward was £10; for stealing cattle, sheep or horses five guineas and for felonies carrying sentences less than transportation it was £2. For all minor offences one guinea was payable.

The existence of a corporation, which had no semblance of democracy, was becoming an increasing affront to the people generally. Even worse, the number of burgesses in Neath had been swollen by non-residents; out of 77 no fewer than 47 lived outside the borough. The day of democratically elected local councils was now at hand. But before this happened, Parliamentary Reform was accomplished by the famous Act of 1832. A large number of the new industrial classes had no parliamentary vote but the Reform Act gave this right to every householder of property worth an annual value of £10. This meant an additional 137 voters to the 42 who already enjoyed the parliamentary franchise. The limited nature of the Act can be seen by remembering that Neath had, at that time, a population of 4,034. Parliamentary reform usually preceded municipal reform and, in 1833, came a Report of the Commissioners appointed by the Whig government who were determined to carry out municipal reform. The Commissioners were young Whig intellectuals who were anxious to highlight the weaknesses of the boroughs to prove the necessity for reform.

There was general agreement that the manorial boroughs had fallen into a confusion during the last century which was almost beyond unravelling. In some of the smaller Welsh Boroughs privileges and functions had long become obsolete. In Prendergast, in Pembrokeshire the only relic of its past as a borough corporation was a mock election of a Mayor, whose qualification was that he had been "oftenest drunk through the year."

The Report of Commission for Municipal Reform on the boroughs that were functioning in some form or other was subjected to criticism for being too abusive and not sufficiently scientific. Yet, as far as Neath was concerned, the facts unearthed justified the nature of the Report.

In October 1833, James Booth, a Young Whig barrister and the Commissioner appointed for this area, arrived in Neath. He immediately proceeded to delve into every facet of the Corporation and its activities. He described the council as consisting of a Portreeve, twelve Aldermen, and eight Capital Burgesses which formed a Common Council. The officers consisted of a Recorder or Town Clerk for which no qualifications were needed and no salary paid. His duties included the keeping of records and recording of the proceedings of the Council. These duties were carried out by the Constable of the Castle who was, therefore, acting in a dual capacity. There were two Common Attorneys, who acted as Treasurers for the corporation and superintended all property transactions. They were paid two guineas per annum. Two Sergeants of the Mace served to attend the Portreeve on official functions and executed judgements of the civil courts but no salaries or fees were payable to these unfortunates. Then there was an officer called a Layer Keeper. His duties were to see that the river was kept free of impediments, floating timber and the like. He also had to inspect the river bridge. No salary was payable but he was comparatively well rewarded for he received six pence for every vessel entering in port. This came to £24 per annum after deductions of expenses. In view of the fact that the Layer Keeper concerned never carried out his duties, it is hardly surprising that there was great resentment at the payments having to be made. It would be interesting to know what some of the ship captains actually said about the matter! The office of Hayward (of ancient manorial history) involved the keeping the town pounds for straying animals. He received four pence for every beast impounded, which brought him, on average, an average income of £20.

Other offices of antiquity were ale tasters and searchers of leather, who were supposed to inspect the quality of the commodities to see if they were up to standard. However, these offices had become merely nominal ones. The town had a crier who was paid half a crown (by the vestry) on the admission of every burgess. The admission of the latter was made by the Aldermen and Common Council. They could elect whom they pleased; no residential qualifications were necessary. The burgesses still enjoyed exemption from tolls and were entitled to 13 "weys" of coal from the lord of the manor at one shilling per load. But this prerequisite had long disappeared.

The Portreeve himself was elected for one year by the Constable of the Castle from three nominations by the Aldermen. He was to preside at the town's local courts to regulate markets and fairs and to act as Deputy Returning Officer. His was easily the most lucrative office of all, for all tolls and port dues went into his pocket, amounting to the very attractive sum of £100, after deduction of expenses. Tolls were payable on each vessel and also on cargoes. Examples quoted were, one penny per container of cheese, four pence per ton of salt and one penny per barrel of herrings. Market and fair tolls were farmed out for £20 annually. Tolls on passing traffic through the town were also payable to the Portreeve such as ten pence for each black cow and one penny for each horse.

The police system, such as it was, consisted of six constables elected by the Portreeve from a body of 12 burgesses nominated by the Alderman. No wages were paid but small fees were payable when warrants were executed. Not unexpectedly, the force was described as "extremely inefficient, often discharging duties reluctantly and without skill." Untrained and largely unpaid, what could anyone expect?

The gaol consisted of four rooms and was described as most unsatisfactory, as there was easy communication with the public from the cells. In 1832, the gaol was sited in James Street, later rebuilt to serve as a joint building for borough and county.

The total income of the Corporation amounted to £142 eight shillings and sixpence which was not a great deal more than the combined emoluments of the Portreeve and Layer Keeper which amounted to £127. The burgesses were excluded from attending any elections or in participating in a business except when they were called in for special reasons. Great dissatisfaction was felt in the town according to the Commissioner, and the general feeling was that all appointments were made to establish the political influence of the present lord of the borough, H. J. Grant. Proof of this lay in the fact that he, himself, his brother and brother-in-law were Aldermen and the Constable of the Castle was his law agent.

But a word of praise for the attorneys was recorded in the report. Formerly, the practice (mentioned earlier in these pages) was for the burgesses to be present at the passing of the accounts of the attorney and all surplus funds were distributed among them. Latterly, this practice had been discontinued as a result of David Powell's action. During the last seven years, a fund had accumulated under the heading "Revenue".

The final comment in the Report of Mr Booth was that the sole practical use of the Borough was to perpetuate the power of the ruling local gentry and to ensure emoluments for a few favoured individuals. It was stated that, in fact, the borough existed for no purpose of general utility. However, in the Corporation Act which followed, Neath was one of 18 boroughs out of 60 Welsh towns visited that was allowed to become known, in future, as a municipal borough.

The last recorded act of the Old Corporation was the mooting of a new market hall. At a Common Hall meeting in September 1834, it was

Coal works in Neath by J. Hassell (1798). *(By permission of the NLW).*

proposed to set up a new market. A report was presented to the effect that the existing market was inadequate to cope with the increasing trade, industry and population. More people from outside were visiting the market and the streets adjoining it were becoming very congested. After a great deal of discussion, it was agreed to ask the clerk, David Powell, to make the initial necessary arrangements for the erection of a new market. In the Hall Day minute book of a meeting in January of the following year, the sum of £500 was given to David Powell for this purpose. A Mr Heycock was instructed to prepare plans and specifications and, eventually, tenders were invited. Three were submitted involving sums of £2,515, £1,180 and £1,650. The lowest tender was accepted, the constructor being W. Whittington. Four canal shares, worth £325 each, were given to the Corporation by H. J. Grant of the Gnoll towards the cost of erection and he also presented the ground to the Corporation by Deed of Gift dated December 18th 1833, part of which land was occupied by the house and shop of Weston Young, and land in possession of William

Powell. A map of 1843, drawn by William Wallace, younger brother of Alfred Russel Wallace, the famous anthropologist, showed that the market had a covered surround for stalls, with four open spaces inside containing stalls in the shape of a cross; adjoining the market was a cattle mart on land bought from Grant, in 1838, for £400, for which Mr Charles Harris was engaged to erect railings and gates. In the Act for the Removing the Market (which received the Royal assent in July, 1838), it was made clear that no produce would be allowed to be exposed for sale outside the market. Any offender would be liable to a fine of forty shillings. But permission would be given for fish, eggs, butter and fruit to be carried in hand baskets from door to door for sale. Another item, which had an echo in a recent controversy relating to Neath Market, stated that any surplus of income from the market was to be "applied to such purposes of public benefit within the said Borough as to the Corporation shall seem to meet."

The street where the old market and Guildhall had been demolished had once been called High Street, a name usually applied to streets which were the main thoroughfares of a town. It then changed to Market Street and, when the new market was erected, it became known as Old Market Street but, such was the confusion between the old and new names with the word "market", that the name Green Street was re-established.

The building was unpretentious enough but contemporary opinion (in Hunt's Directory) described it as a "neat convenient market house . . . and forms prominent feature in modern improvements. The market is well attended and well supplied with various provisions. It is held on Wednesdays and Saturdays, the former being the regular market day."

Various improvements and additions were made in later years, a major one in 1877 being the erection of a complete roof covering. In the big hall, thus created, were held public meetings and eisteddfodau until the building of the Gwyn Hall in 1888. In 1904, the marked was re-built for over a £1,000 which forms the modern market with its somewhat drab frontage. The stalls in the adjoining cattle market were closed despite protests from the stall holders who were, however, offered stalls in the new market.

The River Bridge

The pre-reform days saw, also, another project being completed namely a new River Bridge and a much needed one it was. The old timber bridge of early Tudor times referred to by Leland was described, in an 1683 Court Leet record, as badly needing repair but, such was the state of local government in those days, little or nothing was done and, in 1735, the bridge collapsed. In the account records of Pleydell Courteen, Steward of the Gnoll estates, is a reference to this disaster and the visit he made to the spot with the burgesses of the town and William Gabbs, the Portreeve; a new bridge was built part stone, part timber. The stone part was at the town end, and a timber trestle, with two stone arches, at the Cadoxton end. It was far from being an efficient job for, in 1792, the bridge was described as in a dangerous and ruinous state. A committee was set up (it met in the Ship and Castle Hotel) to plan the erection of a new bridge which would last. The Portreeve was instructed to organise appeals for public subscriptions. Lord Vernon headed the list with a donation of £100 and the various parishes in the district were assessed for contributions. More than one appeal had to be launched before sufficient funds were obtained. The new bridge was designed by David Edwards, son of the famous builder of bridges in Wales, William Edwards.

Of incidental interest is that a Neath man, William Whittington of Melyn-Cryddan, was responsible for the stone bridge at Ynyspenllwch in Glais, in 1805 and the Ynys-y-bont bridge in Crynant. It was he who built Neath market, in 1838.

According to a minute book, in the Neath antiquarian archives, the Neath Bridge was completed in 1801. In later years, alterations were made to level off the bridge to accommodate the Tennant Canal and railway bridge and, in 1869, the bridge was widened by 13ft.

Turnpike Trusts

Before the eighteenth century, the task of keeping the roads in repair was the responsibility of the parish as we have seen. But increasing traffic made this system of obligatory free labour of the parishioners break down.

In 1706, the Turnpike Trusts took over the job of repairing roads. This was based on the principle of making those who used the roads pay for them. A number of landowners and the prominent men would form a Trust (one of the many Statutory Boards which sprung up in the eighteenth century) to be responsible for the roads in their districts. The Turnpike Trust for this area was called the Neath and District Trust and this controlled the roads from Neath to Pontneddfechan. The practice soon began of leasing out the tollgates at a public auction and, in 1805, we find that it resulted in the West Gate (at the junction of Bridge Street and Cadoxton Road) being leased to Nathaniel Miers (the Cadoxton industrialist) for £405, the South Gate (formerly at the end of Gnoll Avenue and, later removed to the bottom of the Cimla Road) and East Gate (Penydre) were leased to James Coke (four times Portreeve of Neath) for one year at a rental of £185. There was also a gate at Pontneddfechan and

Abernant. Usually the lessee was given the rights to erect bars or chains across the roads where tolls would be collected as well as at tollgates. The usual dues collected in 1839, were as follows:

6d = each horse with carriage.
4d = each horse with cart.
1/6 = one score of cattle.
1/- = one score of sheep.

No person should pay at more than three gates from midnight to midnight but this rule was flagrantly broken by lessees by the addition of chains or bars. At first, there was no toll payable on lime, hay, corn or manure which was not for sale, but lime was later added, as it was becoming increasingly used. At the entrance to the present Chain Road at Glyneath (a word with an obvious derivation) there stood a hut where the toll collector stayed from 8 a.m. to 8 p.m. in the execution of his duties. After he left at 8 p.m., local traffic, as one can imagine, increased.

Neath West Tollgate, at junction of Bridge Street and Cadoxton Road. Toll House rebuilt about 1885, removed 1895. *(Reproduced from an old photograph by kind permission of Mrs Stanley Thomas).*

Neath East Tollgate House. Reproduced from an old photograph.
(By permission of the Neath Antiquarian Society).

The story goes that a curate living at Pentreclwyda could be seen regularly each evening passing up to Glyneath in his horse and trap a few minutes after eight to meet his fiancée. Many ways were adopted to dodge this onerous payment of tolls. Goods on which tolls were payable would be covered with hay or straw. Some farmers would unhitch the horse and drag the cart through. Attempts to avoid the gate were thwarted by the Trust, allowing ditches to be dug each side of the gate. The Rebecca Riots, which broke out in 1838, did not touch this area but an elderly inhabitant of this district remembers being told that his grandfather was forced to join a party of followers of Rebecca to smash toll gates in the Vale of Glamorgan. One night, they rode off all dressed in women's clothes but, before they went very far, this person fell from his horse negotiating a ditch. He pretended he was too hurt to go on so the party left him. As soon as they had gone, he scrambled back on his horse and thankfully galloped home. The nearest toll gate smashing to Neath was at Ty-Coch toll gate on the Neath to Swansea road — the two chief leaders of the rioters "Shoni Scwbwr" and "Dai Cantwr" being captured at a nearby farm and, later, transported to Australia.

The first survey of roads in Glamorgan was made in 1789 and surveyors were specially appointed for the task. One reported that of 56½ miles of road in the county 36½ miles were badly in need of repair. In 1827, the famous road engineer, Mr Macadam, was appointed Surveyor General to the Neath and Aberdare Trusts; the assistant surveyor appointed under him was a Mr Kirckhouse of Neath. Although the Rebecca rioters were suppressed, they could claim a victory for, in 1845, Turnpike Trusts were abolished and County Road Boards took over. Tolls still continued in some parts but were finally abolished in 1888, when roads passed to the County Council.

The Manorial Courts

Reference has been made to dominance of the Court Baron under the Mackworths in the eighteenth century. Much of the little business which was done, was the collection of debts due to the lord of the manor. Sometimes, the Court went by the name of the Court Leet and View of Frankpledge, sometimes by the name of Court of Leet and Baron. In the latter years of the century, the Court of Pie Powder is named but the business executed, the little that was, was exactly the same, and there was also the Court of Pleas, which was usually combined with the Pie Powder Court. Besides lists of debtors, details of election of officers appeared periodically. This continued up to 1818, when records were first described as Corporation minutes and the meetings held on "Hall Days". The multiplicity of courts involving the manor, the Borough and the Quarter Sessions of the county, were so inextricably bound up that it was almost beyond any unravelling. Local Government reform was more than overdue.

CHAPTER 8

Neath as a Reformed Borough (1835-1888)

References to Acts of Parliament can seldom be expected to excite anyone but the great Municipal Reform Act of 1835 was of such epoch-making importance that it merits serious attention. It meant, in essence, that for the first time since the Borough was formed, every ratepayer of the town was given the power to elect a council of his own choice. Instead of the "close" corporations of self-elected and adopted members from the so-called elitist class, a democratically elected council took its place. That this revolution took eight centuries to come about is surely something to marvel at. Actually, this Act was more democratic than the Parliamentary Reform Act which preceded it in 1832, which allowed only residents who owned property worth £10 a year to vote. Under the Municipal Reform Act, every ratepayer, who had resided in the Borough for over three years, could vote for the candidate of his choice.

Councillors were to be elected for three years but Aldermen could serve for a term of six years. They were nominated by the council and were not, necessarily, members of it. This was to ensure that experienced public figures could be part of the new corporations.

The new councils were given powers that were very limited, for Parliament was afraid of pursuing the path of reform too hastily. In the administration of finance, the local authority was restricted very rigidly to expend public funds only for community purposes, and auditors were to be elected (not appointed) to ensure proper control. This meant an end to the flagrant misappropriation of corporation revenue which was carried on in so many boroughs. No longer could a transaction take place such as the one recorded in November, 1817, when H. J. Grant was granted a sum of £200 by the Neath Corporation with no interest payable and no reference made to any date of repayment. This was by no means the only case, as the Commissioners noted, for they were minor offences compared to what went on in other towns, such as Berwich-upon-Tweed, where money was borrowed simply for the purpose of sharing it out amongst the burgesses; and, at Leicester, where £10,000 was spent by the Corporation in order to get a certain individual elected and a mortgage was raised on council property to pay the bill. Many corporations believed that they could do what they liked with what they regarded as their own property, and had no compunction in telling the Commissioners that this was good law. At Yeovil, the Portreeve sold the whole of the corporation property at a public auction!

A measure of central control was introduced by the enaction that no loan could be raised or municipal property sold without the consent of the Treasurey but, apart from this, the principle of local autonomy was observed. The council could appoint what staff they pleased but it was obligatory to have a Town Clerk and a Treasurer. They were, also, expected to organise a Police Force through a Watch Committee but this will be dealt with in later pages.

The historic election of the first Council elected by popular vote took place in December 1835 and the "greatest order was maintained from first to last." The following made up the council of twelve:

William Llewellyn	Rees Morgan
Capel Miers	Sankey Gardener
Dr Eliot	Benjamin Howell
James Grainger	Nathaniel Jones
David Arthur	Soloman Bowen
R. P. Leyson	Robert Evans

The Council, later, elected the following as Aldermen:

Henry John Grant
Thomas Dumayne Place
John Rowland
Charles Warde

On the following day, the council met again and elected J. J. Grant, Mayor of the Borough. He was, therefore, the first civic head to be officially designated "Mayor". The leader article in the "Cambrian" emphasised the party political element in ths situation when it referred to "routing the municipal Tories from their strongholds of corruption . . . we shall, we hope, now reap the fruit of our labours in the cause of reform, by the expenditure of the Borough revenues in the improvement of our towns. The Corporation purse will not now be available to pension off an electioneering retainer nor will the Tories be able to bribe the corrupt and degraded freemen with the spoils of the corporation chest".

In Neath, whilst a number of the Aldermen were of the "reform school", the old guard of Grant, Place, Rowland and Wade were still in power and were, in fact, to dominate the chief positions in the council for some time to come. The first four mayors, after the election, were the afore-mentioned Aldermen.

No reference was made in the Act of powers relating to sanitation, water, roads, fire fighting or lighting. The latter had, however, been initiated by the Parish Vestry under the Provisions of the Lighting and Watching Act of 1830. In December 1831, a meeting of the Parish Vestry had taken place, under the chairmanship of the Manorial lord, H. J. Grant (instead of the usual chairman the Rev. H. Knight, Rector of Neath) and it decided that it was fully time that the town should have public lighting. A committee was formed to report on the cost of establishing a gas works. The members consisted of H. J. Grant, the Rev. H. Knight, John Young, Edward Smith and David Powell who became known as "Gas Inspectors." A site was found in the Latt and, in the folowing January the Neath Gas, Light and Coke Co. began to operate, initially under the control of the Parish Vestry. The gas works was completed in January 1833 and fifty lamps were installed. This was 27 years after the first gas lamp appeared in Manchester although Neath was one of the first towns in Wales to be lighted by gas.

In recounting the various utilities set up in the period up to the 1888 Reform Act, we shall find the same confusing multiplicity of authorities as we saw in the previous century. There will be the Parish, the Quarter Sessions, Statutory Boards, Private Companies and the Corporation itself. In the eighteenth century anarchy was made worse by the fact that there was no theory or practice of local government. At least after the 1835 Reform Act, the term "local government" began to be used and a community civic consciousness was developing, however slowly.

Administratively, the problem was to be a lack of co-ordination between the various agents of local government. Even worse was an absence of agreed aims and the bitter antagonism between the "reformers" and those who opposed reform because it would impose a burden on the ratepayers. The clash exists today in varying degrees but then it operated in the context of an appalling lack of sanitation and the dreadful epidemics it produced. Added to the difficulties, was the reluctance of the Government to interfere too much in local government. It failed to force local authorities to implement Health Acts, which were, too often, merely adoptive (or optional).

The most pressing problem was that of Public Health and the related problems of sanitation and a water supply in an age when new houses were springing up to meet the needs of a rapidly expanding population. A brief look at the economic expansion which took place in Neath will make it clear how the problem arose. How the difficulties were solved provides the theme of local administration in the nineteenth century. And a somewhat incredible story it is.

Quaker Domination in 19th Century Neath

Before the development of tinplate and iron industry in Neath in the second half of the century, the most significant feature of the history of the town was the Quaker industrial undertakings in Neath Abbey and the emergence of a personality who was the master brain of these works and was also the leader of many of the moral and social causes of Victorian times. His name was Joseph Tregelles Price of the Society of Friends, popularly known as the Quakers.

Perhaps some reference to the early development of this unique religious sect would illuminate its significance. The freedom from state and church control under Cromwell created an extremely wide variety of Puritan sects which included Independents, Baptists, Unitarian Seekers, Ranters, Diggers and — Quakers. Of these sects Quakers were unique in that they believed in complete equality which led them not to recognise any authority in the Church or state. The founder of this Society of Friends was George Fox, son of a Lincolnshire Weaver, who one day in 1647 experienced a wonderful feeling of being in direct communication with God. This was the 'Inner Light' which led Quakers to describe themselves as 'Children of Light'.

Priests, set prayers, sermons and music were regarded as unnecessary; even the Bible was only a supplement of the truth. To the Quakers all members of the Society of Friends were priests. Burials, baptisms and marriages were conducted without priests. Logically they refused to pay church rates and tithes. It is not surprising that they invoked hostility especially in the Restoration Period when they suffered almost unbelievable persecution. After the Toleration Act of William and Mary, persecution ceased (except distraint for non-payment of Church rates and tithes). Later in the century, Quakers became more outward looking and began to turn to business and commerce. They believed that they could serve God as much in the warehouses as in their Meeting Houses. It was the story of talents. Not to use any was a sin.

The first mention of a Quaker in Neath was in 1749. He was Evan Roberts, an ironworker in High Street, but it was the arrival of the dynamic personality of Evan Rees from Llanidloes that infused the embryonic movement with real vigour. He married Elizabeth Williams of Pontypool who, despite her eleven children travelled widely, preaching the doctrine of Quakerism. Then came an influx of Friends from Cornwall. The families of Fox, Price, Tregelles and Wood decided that

Joseph Tregelles Price (1784-1854), the Swansea Quaker, Industrialist and Moral Reformer.
(By permission of the Library of the Society of Friends, London).

Neath Abbey was an appropriate place to continue and develop clear industrial concerns which they had operated in Cornwall in copper and iron. In Neath Abbey, there were supplies of coal and iron which would enable them to expand. They were all Quakers and the Society of Friends in Neath decided in 1792 to build a Meeting House to accommodate the new membership. A piece of land on the Castle boundary was donated by Moly Leigh (the widow of Sir Robert Mackworth who became the wife of Capel Leigh, the Pontypool industrialist). She came from Quaker stock being the daughter of Nathaniel Miers of Ynys-y-Gernon tinplate works. The Meeting Place that was built is still used as a place of worship, although sadly in need of repair.

Iron furnaces were established at Neath Abbey and Wood was soon replaced by Peter Price who had extensive experience in America in furnace construction. Price married Anna, the daughter of Samuel Tregelles. Large scale production of engines soon took place and in 1806 a coal pit of record depth was sunk in Bryncoch by William Kirkhouse, the canal engineer.

The person who eventually became managing director at Neath Abbey was Joseph Tregelles Price, the son of Peter and Anna Price. Not only did he become the master brain behind all the industrial undertakings but he led the way to a large number of social reforms.

Born in Penrhyn near Falmouth, he was sent to school in Compton but at the age of 14 his father considered that he was sufficiently mature to enter the business at Neath Abbey. In 1817 Tregelles Price, his broker Habberly and two members of the Fox family formed a new company producing iron and engineering goods destined to become world famous for their quality. The undertaking is notable that it provides an early example of integration in industry. Included were two blast furnaces, foundries, engineering shops and from 1825, a shipbuilders yard and a dry dock. Engines from Neath Abbey powered the Dowlais and Cyfartha Ironworks. Mining machinery was exported to Mexico and India and in 1830 a rack and pinion locomotive was supplied to the Pen-y-Derren Ironworks. In 1846 was launched the 'Neath Abbey', the firsh ship to be built of iron in Wales. The ship 'Serena' was the first iron ship to sail round Cape Horn. Blast furnaces were also built in Glynneath where the main source of iron ore was obtained.

It is worth recording that a colliery engine built in 1840 in Neath Abbey was still working perfectly in a colliery in the Forest of Dean in 1923. It was said that it was working with 'beautiful efficiency'.

Tregelles Price was a perfectionist in the typical Quaker mould. The Quakers generally did not believe expanding to any great degree as they feared it might affect the quality of goods. They were also fanatically opposed to manufacturing armaments unlike other ironmasters who made large fortunes in so doing.

Education

The Price family, Peter and his son Tregelles were dedicated to foster education. At first housed in the works, special buildings were later built to house infants, girls and boys departments. Inspectors' Reports spoke highly of all aspects of the Schools.

Temperance

Sobriety was a firm tenet of Quaker belief and Neath became the centre of the Total Abstinence Society. The Quaker Mayor, Councillor Keway paraded the streets each Saturday night denouncing the evils of drink like some modern Savanerola.

Capital Punishment and Penal Reform

This was another cause which the Quakers embraced. Capital punishment to them was a form of judicial murder. In the Merthyr riots of 1831 many of the rebels were arrested and one young man Richard Lewis was accused of wounding a soldier. He was tried and sentenced to death. Tregelles Price was convinced of his innocence and presented a petition of 1000 names (collected in Merthyr) to the Home Secretary and made a personal appearance before him. The execution was stayed for one week but Melbourne, the Home Secretary, was subjected to much pressure from the establishment who feared wide-scale rebellion, signed Lewis' death warrant (he was known as Dic Penderyn from the name of his cottage in Taibach). He has been regarded as a working class martyr ever since; especially since a Merthyr man who escaped to America, confessed to the wounding of the soldier.

Whilst on a visit to Paris, Tregelles Price and his sister Jessica persuaded the French authorities to remove capital punishment for political offences. Whilst in France he helped to create the 'Societe de la morale Christienne'.

Jessica Price, despite ill-health, accompanied her brother on his travels to America and the continent. She was particularly devoted to the cause of penal reform and visited many prisons in this cause. Carmarthen was one prison she visited. Here were imprisoned the Rebecca rioters. Jessica was successful in improving somewhat the deplorable prison conditions there and also in worthy of comparison with Elizabeth Fry, the famous Quaker dedicated to prison reform.

Paternal Capitalism

The Society of Friends were benevolent employers and considered that trade unions were unnecessary if employers exercised scrupulous concern for the welfare of the workers. When the workers of Abbey Iron Works met to form a union at the time of the Merthyr riots, they were dissuaded from doing so by Tregelles Price and his colleagues. The latter failed to realise that all employers did not exercise the same humanitarianism as they did.

Peace Movement

Of all the causes embraced by Tregelles Price the cause of peace was nearest his heart. In a Quaker Salon in Plough Court Pharmacy in Lombard Street, London run by William Allen (of the firm Allen and Hanbury), the first Peace Society in the world was formed with Tregelles Price as its first President. This was in 1816. A year later a branch was formed in Neath, the first Peace Society formed outside London. Such peace societies spread rapidly and several world conferences were held where British and American delegates were prominent.

In the early 1850's politicians like Palmerston were whipping up anti-Russian feeling. Russia was alleged to be intent on invading Turkey. Tregelles Price called a meeting in the Town Hall early in 1854 to advocate the settling of the quarrel by peaceful means but the word of the audience was extremely linguistic and the meeting ended in riotous behaviour during which Price was accused of insulting the Queen. He left the meeting bitterly disillusioned. In December of that year he died. The Society of Friends were strongly opposed to violence of all kinds, even a 'just war' was unacceptable to them. Civil disobedience was the way to combat evils. Anti-slavery was still another cause the Quakers took up. Slavery had been abolished in Britain in 1807 and in 1834 it was ended in the Empire. But in U.S.A., the French Colonies and other places, it still operated and Tregelles Price and his friends never ceased to campaign against what they regarded as the ultimate degradation of the human spirit.

Another Quaker family who directed their energies in commercial activities in Neath were the Redwoods; in particular Isaac Redwood. He built a tannery in Bridge Street, a white building which was a Neath landmark before it was demolished in the early 1950's. He was also one of the friends of the Neath Philosophical Society founded in 1834 together with Tregelles and Nathaniel Price.

Another notable family in the Society of Friends was the Gibbins family. Joseph Gibbins came from Birmingham and, in 1816, opened a bank in Neath with Robert Eaton and William Gronow, and also took over the Melincryddan Chemical Works, later assigning it to his brother Bevington. In 1866 it passed to his son F. J. Gibbins. Eventually, one of his sons Frederick William became the managing director. He became associated with the Eaglesbush Tinplate Works together with his brother Theodore. In 1922, this was sold to the Metal Box Company.

Of the Gibbons family it was Frederick William who was the most prominent. He was founder of the Welsh Plate and Sheet Manufacturing Association, and director of the Landore Steel Factory and a member of the Glamorgan Wages Board.

The decline of Quakers in the 19th century can be attributed to several causes. The land discipline of disownment resulting from marriage outside the Society and disownment owing to business failure tended to sap the vigour of the Society.

The austerity of the Quaker Service drove many members to the non-conformists where music and sermons were colourful attractions. The

Copper works at Neath, 1779, by Paul Sandby. *(By permission of the National Museum of Wales).*

percentage of Quakers attending a place of worship in the latter part of the 19th century was 3.5%. The Society of Friends were a spiritual elitist sect with a permanent image of integrity and humanitarianism. Tregelles Price will remain the outstanding personality of the 19th century. In relation to their numbers the Quakers exercised an extraordinary influence on the industrial and social scene. In the first quarter of the present century this continued. Besides the prominence of F. W. Gibbins and his brother Theodore, in addition to his industrial activities, he was specially interested in antiquarian studies and was President of the Antiquarian Society for many years. With the emergence of representatives from the Trade Unions and Labour Party their influence waned. The defeat of Theodore Gibbins by the late Rev. Degwel Thomas in the 1931 municipal elections was not simply the defeat of a prominent man. It signified the end of an era.

The disciplines of the last century have now been relinquished by the few remaining Quakers who still attend the Friends Meeting House but the humanitarian character of the 19th century Quakers still prevails.

Industrial Development and its Effects

The advent of large ships importing foreign ores meant the decline of Neath River Port and the movement of the copper and iron industries coastwards. Briton Ferry benefitted markedly from this and a rolling mill and blast furnace was set up and, in 1850, the first tinplate works appeared (the Vernon Co.). Rapid population growth was a natural result. Economic expansion in Neath was evident although somewhat slower. It was the coming of the Railways which gave it an impetus. Neath became very much a "railway town" with extensive maintenance sheds. A tinplate works was established in the Melyn which became an extensive source of employment. In Briton Ferry a chemical works grew up by the Copper works at Red Jacket. These were the forerunners of steel and tinplate developments in the 1880's.

The Gnoll enterprises had disappeared and a new elongated strip stretched southwards to Briton Ferry along the river, canal and railway zones. Ribbons of terraced housing followed the industrial growth along the main road and branching out on both sides.

The old Castle area centred in Water Street had been the commercial

Aberdulais Mill, Rheola, by Thomas Horner.
(By permission of the National Museum of Wales).

centre of the town but the new developments drew this southwards. The junction of valley routes, the railway station and the market prevented any major shift and the commercial centre of gravity was now in Green Street, Queen Street and Upper Windsor Road. The Castle became, in the words of Harold Carter, "a submerged area." Between 1850 and 1880 the population of Neath grew rapidly from 5,000 to nearly 14,000.

Socially, it created a prominent working class who, however, profited very little from the new wealth created by the new industrial growth. They were, as elsewhere, exploited in the sacred name of profit. What became evident was a growing, prosperous middle class, wielding considerable power in the community. The majority of councillors were business people but all the higher civic positions (Mayor and Alderman) remained for a long time the prerogative of the professional class, mainly doctors and solicitors, and industrialists. In terms of personalities, a number of names emerge who played a conspicuous part in the government of the town. From the Brick and Tile works there were N. Allen and Thomas Andrews, serving councillors in the 1860's. Sankey Gardner and D. H. Morgan were products of the iron and brass foundries; both these industrialists served as

Mayor and Aldermen. Then there was the brewing industry from which the notable figures of Evan Evans and his son-in-law, David Bevan came. The former began as a shopkeeper and later became an agent for the Guinness company. He then bought the bankrupt Bucklands Brewery of the vale of Neath for £1,250, a twentieth of its value. By the 1860's he not only became a successful brewer but also a colliery proprietor and property owner. Selected town councillor in 1846, he served continuously for 25 years. He was Mayor of Neath in 1856 and 1862. David Bevan, a surveyor and engineer from Cwmavon, married his daughter and followed very much in the footsteps of his father-in-law. A councillor in 1869, he became an Alderman in 1871 and Mayor of the town in 1872 and 1873. He achieved a niche in local government history by being the first Mayor to wear civic regalia which he bought himself. Other public positions he held were Poor Law Guardian and Harbour Commissioner.

There were other industrialists who were not natives of the area such as Williams and Foster of the Mines Royal Copper works at Neath Abbey,

Iron forge near Neath (unknown). *(By permission of the NLW).*

Copper smelting inside the Abbey walls in 1791 by Roe and Co. (later named Cheadle Co.). A classic case of industrial vandalism.

Leach and Flowers of the Melyn works (who were the largest employers of labour in Neath) and Morwood of Baglan Tinplate Company. Banking and insurance managers were a class which also emerged with industrial development, but the group which had consistently occupied the leading roles in public affairs were drawn from the religious, legal and medical category.

A leading figure in the Parish Vestry and many Town organisations was the Rector of Neath, the Rev. H. Knight, scholar, editor and antiquary. He was an enormously respected figure in the town. He retired to his family home in Newtown in 1855 and was succeeded by the Rev. John Griffiths who achieved similar public status. He served on many boards and became deeply involved in the public life of Neath. He was a brilliant preacher in Welsh and English and a constant visitor to his parishioners. He constantly urged the more happy-go-lucky to be organised and thrifty and he became known as "Shon Trefan". Three doctors, R. P. Leyson, James

French and W. G. Jones spent many years on the Town Council. Of similar status were Alexander and Howel Cuthbertson and Henry Pendrill Charles, prominent solicitors in the James Coke (1766-1835) mould. The latter had established a tradition of solicitor-politician in Neath. Coke became a councillor in 1802 and, after a period out of office, he returned and became an Alderman in 1805. He served as Portreeve four times, in 1810 and in three successive years 1818, 1819 and 1820. His son, H. S. Coke, became Town Clerk in 1839 on the death of David Powell in whose firm he had been employed. Coke resigned in 1866 and was succeeded by his younger partner, Alfred Curtiss, the first of three generations of the Curtiss family who were Town Clerks of Neath. Incidentally, H. S. Coke's son continued the family traditions by becoming Town Clerk of St Pancras.

The Struggle for Sanitary Reform

Perhaps one of the reasons why local Government seldom excites interest is that, so often, it becomes preoccupied with earthy subjects such as sanitation. The details are, however, not so much boring as revolting as will be seen in the pages that follow.

The Parish had, in the past, been responsible for highways and drains but the overseer had always been reluctant to do anything very much because of the tight rein kept on the Parish purse by the Vestry authority. The Corporation, therefore, tended to take over the responsibility for street scavenging but this was done in a far from satisfactory manner. The problem of sanitation, in any case, involved much bigger issues; these were the devastating epidemics of cholera which swept the town in 1849, 1854 and 1866. The worst was in 1849, when 730 people died, 245 inside the Borough. Deaths were not confined to the poorer areas. Dumayne Place, of Ffrwd Vale, a former Mayor and the serving Mayor, Robert Leyson, his nephew, were among the victims. Small pox and scarlet fever were of equal concern, especially the return of small pox and typhus in 1871 which resulted in an appalling death rate. The incidence of deaths was particularly high in areas where malnutrition and poor sanitary conditions were particularly prevalent. In 1866, no less than 520 deaths occurred from cholera.

It would not be difficult to imagine the difficult and dangerous nature of the work of doctors during these epidemics. In at least two instances, public tributes were paid to them. At Glyneath, Dr Brodie fell a victim to cholera in 1851 and, on a tablet in Capel-y-bont where he was buried, the following words were inscribed "This tablet is erected by the inhabitants of the district in grateful remembrance of him who during days and nights of dire pestilence strove with unflinching courage and unremitting attention to mitigate the suffering of his patients and, at last, lost his own life in this service. In February 1867," Dr Charles Pegge, of Briton Ferry, was the recipient of a public presentation in appreciation of the magnificent dedicated service which he rendered during the 1866 outbreak of cholera.

The full story of these epidemics is yet to be told. One story recorded by an elderly lady was that she remembered her grandmother telling her that no one, apart from doctors, was allowed to enter the houses of victims of the plague, so neighbours, anxious to help, used to pay visits very late at night.

Infected water supply was a major contributing factor and drainage from primitive cesspools made serious pollution inevitable. Many of the worse areas were in the older part of the town around the castle. Here were groups of cottages without any form of sanitation except a crude communal convenience. They included places such as Savour's Court, Francis Court and Castle Court.

The situation was not helped by the low personal standards of some sections of the public. In 1854, Superintendent Lyn, the newly appointed Police chief, reported that tallow candles were used on the market stalls. On some butchers' stalls, he found candles stuck in the meat! This, he claimed, was both unhygienic and dangerous. He strongly advised having lighting for the market which was already operating in Swansea. Alderman Kenway fully supported the Superintendent and also deplored the apathy of the market committee. An amusing example of the Alderman's fanatical approach to problems was his suggestion that a policeman should be placed at the door when the market committee met to prevent members leaving before the business was concluded.

The national figure behind the agitation for Neath reform was, of course, Edwin Chadwick who was largely responsible for the Poor Law. The Amendment Act of 1834 had not only placed the Poor Law on a new footing but also exposed the sanitary conditions of the towns. A report, in 1842, eventually led to the famous Health Act of 1848, which provided a complete code of health reforms. Its weakness lay in the fact that its provisions were compulsory only in a very limited sense, but a series of inspections were made under the Act which revealed such shocking conditions that some Councillors became deeply concerned about the need for sanitary reform. A letter in the "Cambrian" (in March 1858) provided hair-raising details about the sanitation in Neath. "In 476 dwellings, containing a total of 2,142 persons, there were no provisions of any sort for water closets or cesspools whilst a further 202 houses, with 947 persons, there were only 40 privies and nearly all in such a state as to be unuseable. Over half the population were in a daily state of discomfort and degradation".

Under the 1848 Health Act, authorities with mortality figures of over 23 per thousand, were obliged to carry out the main provisions of the Act which included adequate drainage sewage and water supplies. Neath was certainly included in this category for its mortality figures were as high as 27 per thousand. A comparison with Merthyr (25.7), Cardiff (20 per 1000) and Swansea (17 per 1000) provided a startling picture of the terrible state prevailing in Neath.

The Nuisance Removal and Disease Prevention Act of 1848 and Lodging House Act of 1851 obliged the council to carry out some limited work in preventing nuisances in public places and dwellings, but this was only the outer fringe of the problem. The distrust felt towards government interference, was very entrenched, due largely to emotional prejudice. The opposition to Centralism and all the alleged dangers of bureaucracy found its most passionate spokesman in Toulmin Smith, who wrote with eloquence and passion on the subject. His philosophy was that local government must be free of statutory controls and should rely upon customary and common law to fulfil local needs. Man had it in his power to supply all his wants without state direction. There was nothing, he argued, which the Parish could not do, if it only made use of its ancient powers. Whilst there might have been an element of truth in this when applied to a small rural parish, the same cannot be applied to the congested new industrial areas.

There was another problem which was to prove far more formidable. That was the question of where the money was coming from to pay for adequate water supplies, sewerage and drainage. It is a question which accompanies most measures of reforms and will, one supposes, always be asked. A rate levy obviously, was necessary because the surplus from the Corporation Fund was pitifully small. Even as late as 1872 it was only £224. But there was already a poor rate, a highway rate and a gas rate levied through the agency of the Parish Vestry and the Council decided that, rather than add another rate, that a loan would be raised.

There was no question that the state of housing up to 1855 was exceedingly poor. The speculative building, which resulted in hundreds of terraced houses being built in the southern part of the town, had not yet got under way. There were large numbers of eighteenth century cottages, many of which were houses built for miners in the old Gnoll Collieries, in a very dilapidated state.

What made matters infinitely worse was the mass poverty that existed in the town. It was so pronounced that nearly half the residents were excused payment of rates. Up to 1842, women and young children worked in the pits and it was poverty that drove them to this. Legislation in the 1840's made this illegal but, as late as 1858, we find that James Penrose,

New Floating Docks, Briton Ferry, from the *London Illustrated News*. *(By permission of the National Library of Wales).*

the Glyneath and Cwmgarwch Colliery proprietor, was charged with employing a boy under ten in Maesmarchog colliery. The foreman who employed him, pleaded that he did so out of sympathy for the family and at the bequest of the father who was sick and had a large family of small children. They were desperately poor. A fine of £5 was imposed.

By 1859, houses were beginning to be built but not one was provided with sanitary facilities. Some were in blocks of twelve and sixteen without a single privy, with no water supplies and the existing drainage system was largely dependent upon two brooks which ran through the town. In the north, the Gnoll Brook and, in the south, the Cryddan Brook provided a natural and open culvert drainage. The responsibility for sanitary control passed from the Parish to the council under the 1848 Act and a new system of drainage and sewage disposal was considered and plans were drawn up. The first act, however, was the providing of access to the River for drainage from the notorious Green Area. A culvert under the canal in 1849 accomplished this, and a new sewer was installed at a cost of £400. In

1852 the District Road Board took over responsibilites and, immediately, drew up plans for a comprehensive system of deep drainage for the town in 1860; but the scheme was abandoned as the Board lacked borrowing powers. Why it should have been given powers without the means to execute them is one of the mysteries of local government of the time.

The Council was now offered the scheme and, in 1865, a new interest in sanitary reform seem to have been created, for the provisions of the new Sewage Disposal Act were adopted and the main part of the scheme was carried out at a cost of £10,500. The Mayor, Pendrill Charles, had played a prominent part in this and so had the older "reform" members like Howel Gwyn, Sankey Gardner and W. G. Jones, who were now immensely gratified at the turn of events.

It was in the same year that, in a January meeting of the Council, a code of bye-laws were issued "for the good rule and government of the Borough, and for the suppression of nuisances therein". A fine of £2 was to be levied on:

1. Every occupier of a house or any building who neglected to sweep and clean all pavements and footways abutting upon the premises and also to clean all water courses.
2. Every person who throws or deposits in any receptacle any manner of rubbish in the street previously to the arrival of the scavenger's cat at the door.
3. Every person who shall beat or shake any carpet, rug or mat or soot bags (except door mats which had to be done before eight o'clock in the morning) in the street.
4. Every person who sells or exposes for sale any putrid meat, fish or any other matter.
5. Every person who neglects an Order from the surveyors or sanitary inspector to prevent any water being deposited on public roads.
6. Every person who shall empty any privy or cesspool between six in the morning and twelve at night or shall use a cart for conveying same without a cover.

Apart from these "heath provisions" the bye-laws included a list of punishable offences relating to the distribution of any profane or obscene literature or ballads, or indulging in games in the street which would injure or annoy the public or cause any danger by "riding or driving furiously in the streets". The proper control of horses by adequate harness was detailed. Prostitutes who loitered or were in any thoroughfare or public place for the purpose of prostitution or being there for the purpose of solicitation, would be subject to the same fine.

It is ironic, to say the least, that, at a time when there was bitter opposition by a majority of the council to the provision of sewerage and water supplies despite cholera epidemics, the shaking of a door mat at the wrong time was a punishable offence.

Water Supplies

The provision of an adequate water supply was the fundamental basic need. Not only was it vital for domestic needs but it was essential for the operation of a sewerage system.

Water for the town came from streams, public and private pumps and the canal. Most of these sources were polluted in varying degrees. An offer came from the steward of the Gnoll Estate, Bullock Webster, of a supply of pure water from the Gnoll Ponds, for which the Corporation was to pay £100 as an annual rental. But, although the majority of councillors were "reformers", it was referred back to the public for a decision. A meeting in 1856, under the chairmanship of Alex Cuthbertson threw it out as it would

Gnoll House, by Neath, 1848. *(By permission of the NLW).*

be too heavy a financial burden. There was popular support for this action from the poorer ratepayers many of whom had been brought into the "ratepaying" category by a new valuation. The next move came from the solicitors of the Gnoll Estate, Ward Osborne and Co. who formulated the idea of a private water company as there seemed little prospect of the Council taking any action. Many of the "reform" Councillors joined in and the Neath Water Company was established with Howel Gwyn as chairman and James Kenway, J. H. Rowland and others, together with the Town Clerk J. S. Coke, becoming directors. The Council, under the mayor, Alex Cuthbertson, was determined to have nothing to do with the company. In fact, the anti-reforming element in the council became stronger. The group consisting of Philip Davies, Richard Walters and W. T. Morgan were now joined by members of the "Popular Party", Richard Bartlett, W. Morris and John Lewis. Election posters of the time reflected popular feeling against reform which had become synonomous with a rise in rates. This feeling persisted until the late 1860's. The posters were written in eighteenth century lampoon style, Evan Evans being referred to as "Double Stout" and Walters, the chandler as "Tallow Dip". The public were warned that fantastic rates would result if "reform" candidates were elected. The Town Clerk, A. Curtiss, (who succeeded H. S. Coke in 1866) was "Albert Slender" or "Albert Longshanks", described as "Clerk of the Course" in the "Corporation Races", whilst P. Flower as "Blighted May Flower". This sort of attack was carried on inside the Council Chamber for a time, Philip Davies referring to Howell Gwyn and R. H. Miers as "The Squire of Dyffryn and his man Friday".

In the meantime, the Water Company had encountered financial difficulties and new working capital was needed. This was, eventually, supplied by a firm of London financiers, J.J. and H. White, and it resulted in a virtual take over of the Water Company in 1868, which now became involved with a Briton Ferry Extension Scheme. The passing of the new Health Reform Acts of 1872 and 1875 and further epidemics, now began to alter the attitude of the public and the council; one difficulty was the quality of the water which was described as "liquid manure".

An attempt was made in 1874, to buy up both the Gas and Water Companies, but, owing to opposition from the Water Company, it succeeded only with the gas. However, the council managed to insist on better and larger supplies from the Gnoll, including filter beds. Later developments of the water supplies included the building up of the Moss House Reservoir in 1897 and the Cefn Cwrt Reservoir at Briton Ferry, but it was the supply from the Ystradfelte Reservoir of the Rural District Council that finally solved the problem. In 1868, the first rate was levied by the Corporation (one shilling in the £) and further extensions of the

sewerage layout took place. By 1879, only 130 dwellings remained unsewered. It could be said that all the main provisions of the 1875 Health Act, apart from the provisions of adequate hospital facilities, had been carried out: whether they had been adequately carried out was another matter. Anyway, a decrease in the very high mortality rates of 27 per 1000 to 21 per 1000 in 1875-8 was proof that some impact, at least, had been made. In 1835, there had been only three officials appointed, the Town Clerk, the Treasurer and Police Inspector. By now, a number of others had been added such as the Medical Officer of Health, a District Surveyor and an Inspector of Nuisances and a number of minor offices.

This drawing was by an unknown artist of the last century. The place of crossing of the Neath River can only be guessed at and the construction of the bridge can only be wondered at. *(By permission of the NLW).*

The change in popular feeling towards reform, due partly to an increase in prosperity in the late 1860's, resulted in many of the "Popular Party" candidates losing their seats. Only Richard Bartlett survived. He had broken away from his early associates and joined the Ratepayers Protection Society which made him welcome. In 1877 he was elected mayor.

The demand for reform was to come from all groups on the council, consequent upon a new public willingness to pay for amenities necessary to any civilised community; but, even more so, because panic about epidemics (there had been another one of devastating proportions in 1870, of cholera and small pox) was to prove greater than fear about rates. The problem had been further eased by the introduction of grant-in-aid and the provision of new rates of interest from the Public Works Loans Board. The setting up of a Local Government Board and the codification of all previous health legislation in the 1875 Act made local authorities responsible for all aspects of public health.

Speculative housing was spreading and, in 1873, the council issued a comprehensive code of bye-laws in an attempt to ensure decent standards in the new buildings and streets. The bye-laws were with "respect to the level, width and construction of new streets, buildings and the sewerage thereof".

The width of streets, the provisions of footways, and of adequate entrances were detailed and it was made clear that the Surveyor of the local authority would specify the materials and plans for the proper drainage of the streets.

Every aspect connected with the building of houses and other premises was set out in great detail, structure, materials, drainage, sewerage, height of buildings, ventilation and light and adequate spacing. These would rigidly be controlled by the authority. One would like to think all these bye-laws were implemented, but, certainly, a big step forward had been made in building and planning control.

New personalities had now appeared on the council such as David Evan Bevan, J. H. Rowland (banker), H. Curtiss (jeweller and brother of the Town Clerk) and James Kempthorne. J. H. Rowland (a leading figure in banking) became particularly prominent, serving as mayor on four occasions (1868, 1871, 1879 and 1880). He became High Sheriff of the County in 1889, and a founder Alderman of the new county council. His daughters became public benefactors after his death in 1899. A prominent industrialist, P. W. Flower of Melyn Tinplate works had a somewhat short tenure of office on the council, from 1869 to 1875, when he resigned. Pressure on his employees to support him in election was a factor in his unpopularity. Other industrialists like George May (chain manufacturer of the Green) and Alex Routledge (signal manufacturer) became, with Richard Bartlett, an effective force in the Ratepayers Association. They became not so much opposed to rates as concerned with their proper use. George May, and Edward Strange Parsons (referred to in the satirical Election poster as "May Fever" and "Strange Parsons") were active in ideas which went beyond matters of drainage and sewerage. A free library and public parks were amenities which they began to advocate. But the need for sanitary reform had been a driving force towards municipalisation and the preoccupation with this had obliterated other more aesthetic ideas. Mrs Humphrey Ward, the Victorian novelist, was to remark, "In my youth we talked about Ruskin. Now we talk about drains". It is recorded that Lytton Strachey once said of Florence Nightingale's passion for sanitation that she was inclined to confuse the Diety with drains, which was a somewhat characteristically unkind remark of Strachey's. Yet it is true of towns in this county that they can be unfavourably contrasted with many towns on the continent where a necessary attention to drainage and such matters certainly did not preclude a development of cultural life, as it should be.

The Police and Law and Order

We have seen that the state of the police force, as the Commissioners found it, was in a very poor shape indeed. The old system of Watch and Ward had proved completely inadequate with the growth of population in the industrial towns.

A new system had been set up in 1829 by Sir Robert Peel but it was to remain under local control. And that was the big mistake. Many of the new corporations like Neath showed little aptitude or desire to establish an efficient force. In 1837, there was only one serving officer, David Prothero, who was paid partly out of the rate for lighting and partly by private subscription. In 1844, the Borough and County had a combined gaol in James Street and the force was increased to two. There were rapid changes in the staff due, almost certainly, to unattractive conditions, the multiplicity of duties being one factor.

In the Watch Committee Minute Book of 1844, the conditions govern-

The opening of the Neath/Swansea Railway from the *London Illustrated News.*
(By permission of the N.L.W.)

ing the duties of officers were set out and busy men they must have been. The Borough was divided into two beats and each policemen had to cover his every half hour. Special attention had to be paid to inns and taverns, to common lodging houses (a list of vagrants had to be kept) and to prostitutes. The supervision of the market and all its regulations was a police duty. Most people kept a pig in those days and many were left to wander round the streets, prevention of which was a special instruction to the unfortunate police officer.

There were two restrictions on the policeman's personal freedom. He was not allowed to leave the town whilst off duty without special permission and he was not permiteed to wear civilian clothes. An advertisement in 1849 seems to suggest an improvement. "A policeman wanted in Neath, wages seventeen shillings per week with clothes and a cottage free of rent". Both the County and the Borough kept a chief officer in the James Street premises but there is no information how the rooms were shared out. In 1852, a new step was taken by the appointment of Superintendent John Worman, at a salary of £80 per annum. He was succeeded by Superintendent Lyn in 1857, and a stormy tenure of office ensued until his retirement in 1860. Lyn took his duties very seriously but, at times, he carried things too far and was often accused of roughhandling members of the public.

On May 14th 1858, Lyn wrote a letter to the Council which showed his concern for the welfare of the town and the lack of concern on the part of the council. He pointed out that there was not a single public convenience of any sort in the town. He also stressed the urgent necessity of a new fire engine. The buckets of the existing one were broken, the hose was unusable and the engine was used as a hen-roost! And what did the council do? They deferred the matter. The Superintendent's plea for additions to the force to cope with growing problems of law and order was also deferred. A peculiar comment ended the press report to the effect that there was nothing of public interest brought before the council; a species of journalistic sarcasm, perhaps.

The measure of Superintendent Lyn's civic consciousness can be also seen in his proposal to the Watch Committee in May 1866, that in consequence of the alarming appearance of cholera, particularly in the area of the port, that a supply of lime and lime brushes and also chloride of lime should, as a sanitary measure, be provided for to purify the drains and gutters and to cleanse the houses of the poorer inhabitants. Lyn achieved his purpose and the committee decided to distribute supplies of chloride of lime and Macdougall's disinfectant powder under the supervision of the Mayor and Superintendent Lyn.

John Phillips took over from Lyn and served until 1888, but, during the whole of the time since the inception of the Force there had been a big turnover in personnel. Much of this was due to dismissals of officers for drunkenness but understaffing and a multiplicity of duties were other reasons. By 1864, there were a superintendent, one sergeant and two constables. The force was increased in 1899 by the addition of another sergeant and eight constables but, by that time, the population had doubled.

The Minutes of the Watch Committee during the period 1844 to 1870 revealed that the Committee had a comic obsession concerning police uniform. In meeting after meeting, long discussions took place on details of clothing; the type of cloth, the kind of buttons, the cut of the coat and trousers, and the shape of the hat and great coat. Whenever any new item was added, the officers had to parade round the council chamber for inspection. If the same dedication was shown to necessary factors affecting the welfare of the town, Neath would have become a model borough.

Social factors, resulting from a rapid rise in population from 1860, produced many stresses and strains. Immigrant labour from Ireland, Devon and Cornwall and also from the adjacent agricultural counties of Pembroke and Carmarthen, hardly made for any social coherence. The language factor also contributed to this situation. Court cases of affrays, particularly between Neath and "Devon men", were recorded. Yet there were very few serious crimes committed. By far the most cases were drunkenness and allied offences such as common assault, various breaches of the peace and evasions of the licence laws.

Murders resulted in public hangings in Swansea up to 1860. At these macabre events, great crowds of up to 30,000 congregated and local shops sold grim souvenirs of the hangings. At a double execution in March 1858, an anti-capital punishment organisation distributed their leaflets amongst the crowd.

Drunkenness in Neath generated an organisation devoted to temperance reform. It certainly had sufficient material to work upon. There were great numbers of taverns of all kinds, 57 in all. Many gin shops giving the town, in Water Street area, a real eighteenth century "Hogarthian" character and even police officers were only too ready to imbibe. A favourite drink was "three pennyworth of cheap brandy". The Temperance Society was, in the main, the product of the non-conformist section of the community which was growing rapidly in the town, with the Independents leading with 41% of all those attending a place of worship.

A Total Abstinence Society was formed in 1858, which several prominent Quakers, such as Joshua Richardson and James Kenway, joined. It was typical of the Rector, the Rev. John Griffiths, that he joined, as he was always ready to ally himself with any sect or denomination if he considered the cause was a good one. Neath soon became the centre of the temperance movement in South Wales. Lectures and meetings were arranged on a wide scale. In April 1858, the "Cambrian" reported the staging of a satirical comedy in the Gwyn Hall entitled, "The Trial of John Barleycorn". The latter was depicted as a farmer who was put on trial for indulging too freely in the evils of alcohol. Evan Evans, Alderman and brewer, staged a counter blast by employing a brass band to play fortissimo outside the all during the "trial". The whold business hardly made for law and order and there was much horseplay. The public, however, thoroughly enjoyed it.

James Kenway was elected Mayor in that year and he certainly made history by his conception of his office as Mayor and chief magistrate. Convinced that drink was the "root of all evil", he was determined to prosecute to the full all cases of drunkenness. One notable case brought a sentence which was probably unique in the whole county at that particular time. One of the "characters" in the town was a prostitute popularly known as "Betsi Creppo" whose house was nothing but a brothel. On June 24, (1859) the following appeared in the "Cambrian":

> 'The punishment or incarceration in the stocks has been almost obliterated in this county as being incompatable with modern notions of justice. Still, few will deny that being held up to public scorn and derision for 3 or 4 hours is a most effective cure for drunkenness. In Swansea, there are no stocks but in Neath there are, and, what is more, they are made use of. One instance occurred last week of a most abandoned and worthless prostitute, a thorough disgrace to her sex, who was fined five shillings and seven shillings and sixpence costs for drunkenness in the streets. In default, she was sentenced to be placed in the stocks for six hours. The name of this woman was Elizabeth Ann Parker, better known as Betsi Creppo, and her drunken propensities had repeatedly brought her efore the bench. On the occasion referred to, a short time was given to her to pay the fine and costs, but nothing whatever was seen of her until a day or two since. She was then found drunk and disorderly in the streets and the police accordingly proceeded to carry out the former sentence of the court. She was placed in the stocks in the market place. Some there were who cried, "Shame!" but did they remember the character of the defendant and that she had disregarded every other method made to reclaim her, they would surely have imagined that, even a few hours of public exposure was not too bad for one who was stated by the police to be a perfect pest to society.'

There was, of course, no condemnation of the men who consorted with these prostitues.

The latest mention of stocks being used elsewhere in the country was in 1852, at Cowbridge. In Neath, there is no record of the stocks being used after the above quoted cases in 1859, but a Victorian traveller, J. W. King, in his wanderings in England and Wales, had written in 1856, as follows:

> 'What the end of these things will be, (a reference to the dispute about the levying of a church rate) and when, I have not been able to gather. It appears that, anticipating something of this kind, the vicar had the old stocks removed and replaced them with new ones. And there they are, close under the church in the grave-yard. If we could but wait, in all human calculation, a few days will see those holes occupied by the brown gaitered legs of a Friend, the carpet-footed legs of a draper and the top-booted legs of a butcher, all martyrs to the exaction of the church rates. As everyone's teeth is set at their neighbour, we are inclined to go out of town.'

King evidently thought that the rector of Neath, the Rev. John Griffiths, of revered memory, would have placed those who opposed the church rates in the stocks. Hardly a credible view!

Two years later, a newspaper report by a journalist who visited St Thomas Church read as follows:

> 'At my left, on emerging from the door opposite to that which I entered, stood the stocks, a relic of the days of the Cooking Stool, which has not yet fallen into disuse.'

In the "Cambrian" of April 1st 1859, it was stated by a correspondent that "the tippler is uniformly fined the drunkard's penalty of five shillings and costs, or six hours in the stocke." The reference to the market place in the first report, must surely have been an error. If not, why and by whom were the stocks removed?

Prostitution in Neath was, undoubtedly, very prevalent in the town duing the 1850's and 1860's. In the year following the sentence to the stocks by James Kenway, Margaret Davies described as "Hall Keeper and Female Searcher" was fined for disorderly conduct. It was reported that she went, in a drunken state, to the house of Betsi Creppo with a number of men. One can only wonder at the standard of the police force when its "female searcher" was of this type. At a later date, a Mary Ann Lewis was sent to prison for two months for being a public nuisance. This person kept a brothel in Duck Street. Another well-known prostitute in the town was one Agnes Davies, who went by the picturesque name of "Swallow Tail". She was, on one occasion, accused of drunken behaviour but, with tearful eloquence, persuaded the Mayor that she would never again "tough the vile trash of beer and spirits" and was let off with a reprimand by a somewhat credulous Bench. Prostitution became so blatant that at a meeting of the Watch Committee in April 1865 with the mayor, Pendrill Charles in the chair, it was reported that a Mr P. Davies had written a complaint regarding a public nuisance; it was that a number of prostitutes were in the habit of patrolling the streets in the neighbourhood of the Wesleyan Chapel and "misconducting themselves on Sunday about the time of divine service". The Superintendent of Police stated "that he himself and the rest of the Police Force were doing all in their power to prevent this nuisance as far as it was possible to do so."

Poverty has often been a contributory cause of prostitution and there was certainly a great deal of poverty in the town especially in the 1850's. As far as the Police were concerned, they were inadequate to deal with public nuisances of any kind, owing chiefly to understaffing.

James Kenway, in his role of "Mayoral Savonarola", was also severe on vagrancy and sentenced wandering beggers to terms in the House of Correction as "rogues and vagabonds" in true eighteenth century style.

That the Parish was killed off by the Poor Law Amendment Act of 1834 under which the Board of Guardians took over the administration of the Poor Law, is a generally accepted fact. S. and B. Webb referred to the death of the Parish in the Metropolitan areas although some of the provincial parishes lingered on in a very attenuated form. Tate, author of an authorative work on the Parish, states that it is possible that parish records came to an end with the passing of the 1834 Act.

In Neath, however, the Parish survived in anything but an attenuated form and a substantial number of Vestry books exist testifying to the fact that the Parish carried a wide variety of activities into the latter part of the century. At times, meetings were described as meetings of ratepayers held in the Town Hall, convened by the Churchwardens. Others were the more conventional vestry meetings. The former was obligatory by law before a rate was levied. To illustrate the extent of the Parish interest we must refer to a meeting of the parishioners in 1837, when it was decided to buy a fire engine for £5, the money to be taken from the proceeds of the Poor Rate! Complaints were recorded, in Vestry minutes of 1843, of the time taken by the fire engine to reach a fire in Rheola and it was decided to investigate the complaints. Attempts made by the Parish authorities to persuade the council to take over the fire services but were of no avail. Evidently, it was beyond the ability of the Parish to cope with the situation for in April

1859, a "Cambrian" press report describes a very sorry state of affairs. The fire engine, it said, was but an apology for one. "In a corner of the corn market securely railed round, stands which, we presume, was once a fire engine, but what it is now is open to speculation. The hose is completely rooted away and so is the woodwork. The fire buckets had long disappeared". Fires must have been dealt with by the centuries old method of householders running with buckets of water from whatever source was at hand. Representatives from a number of insurance companies (such as the "Atlas" and "Norwich Union") offered to contribute towards the cost of a new fire engine. Eventually, the corporation woke up to the necessity for this and made their own contribution of £50. A trained fire officer was, later, appointed and, in 1884, a code of instructions was issued for the police force which included a section relating to the operation of a fire service. Superintendent Lyn's plea of 1858 was at last answered.

The levying of a Church rate for the maintenance of the church soon began to invoke much opposition. Successive demands for its abolition were made by non-conformists like Sankey Gardner and James Kenway who objected "to supporting a religion which they did not believe in". But the voting always went against them. In 1852, a rate collection of £351 fourteen shillings and sixpence was made by the rate collector, Mary Rees, for which she was paid £8 fifteen shillings and sixpence. By 1865, however, the rate was abandoned in the face of the continued opposition, and an attempt was made to organise a voluntary rate of fourpence in the pound. In 1868, the compulsory church rate was continued at a very reduced sum such as a penny half-penny in the pound.

Although the Guardians had now the responsibility of the Poor Law administration it was the Parish who levied the rate but on their instructions. A typical entry in the vestry minutes was that of September 1851. The collector was ordered to collect arrears before the new rate was collected. A levy of a half-penny in the pound was made to meet the demands of the Guardians; this was to be signed by the Justices. So there were three bodies involved which was typical of the confusion of local administration in the nineteenth century. There were frequent references to arrears which reflected the poverty of the town in the mid-century. Every vestry meeting produced its list of householders who were to be exempted from payment of rates. The poor rate continued to be levied by the Parish up to 1912. Sometimes there was a clash between the Parish and the Guardians. In 1859, the relieving officer of the Guardians (who had replaced the overseer) was asked to appear before the vestry to explain certain payments to paupers. He refused.

The gas rate was also a responsibility of the Parish. Not only that, but the financial accounts were in their hands. Vestry minutes record rates levied and accounts submitted from the Gas Company Inspectors who were in the main, the Churchwardens. This continued until the Corporation bought over the gas undertaking in 1874. In addition, a highway rate had to be levied on the instructions of the Highway. In 1871, a rate of nine pence in the pound was levied to raise a sum of £600 for the Highway Board. An attempt at simplifying the whole business was made in May 1861, when William Morris agreed to collect all rates.

Added to these public services, the responsibility lay, of course, with the vestry for the maintenance of the church fabric and also for the administration of the church. To this must be finally added the establishment of the Alderman Davies' School and the responsibility of meeting its running expenses. Previous to this, it was the business of administrating the Mera Charity School that rested on the shoulders of the Churchwardens.

The Parish cannot be left without some reference to the setting up of Llantwit Cemetery, as this was a contribution to the general health of the town. Before the cholera epidemic of 1849, the main burial place in the town was in St Thomas Churchyard and this was becoming overstocked to the point of it becoming a health hazard. (There was limited accommodation in a few Non-conformist Chapels but these were largely confined to their own members.) The scare prompted the Corporation to approach the Rector, the Rev. H. Knight, to discuss whether any solution could be found. A limitation to burials was the only result of this meeting but, in 1860, all burials were stopped by order of the Privy Council with the exception of vaulted graves. This resulted in a very short time in the opening of a cemetery on glebe land in Llantwit.

Before a survey of this period from 1835 to 1888 is complete, the story of gas must be taken up and two other agencies of local government be considered namely, the Board of Guardians and Quarter Sessions.

Gas

We have, earlier in this chapter seen how the idea of gas lighting in the town was first mooted by the Parish Vestry followed by the formation of the Neath Gas and Coke lighting of the town in 1833 with fifty lamps for public lighting. A brief description of the further development of this service must now be made. The old site in James Street was in 1862, replaced by a new position in the Millands and a new works erected there by John Vickary. There was now a big industrial demand for a supply of good and cheap gas. A temporary shortage of capital was solved and, under the chairmanship of Howel Gwyn, the position improved some-

View of Neath published in the *Illustrated London News*, 12 September, 1857.

what, but not sufficiently, to prevent the formation of a new Company. A very confused situation followed then with two companied in existence, with the new company eventually gaining control in 1871. But complaints against the general inefficiency of the gas supplies continued. Under the Health Act of 1872, the Corporation placed by a gas undertaking in 1874 for the sum of £30,000. A new manager, Mr R. A. Browning was appointed, and a period of rapid development ensued. Profits rose and in 1910, a tribute from the press appeared, in which it was pointed out that a sum of £1,000 had been, for some years past, paid back into the rate account.

It is all the more surprising, therefore, to find that, in 1914, there were rumours of inefficiency and even corruption in the gas department. A public meeting was demanded which all members of the council were asked to attend. Nothing tangible, however, emerged. Much of these rumours of corruption emanated from an extremely eccentric character in the town by the name of C. R. Truman. Over a number of years he launched scurrilous attacks on certain members of the Town Council.

Libel and slander actions resulted and Truman served terms of imprisonment arising out of these.

In 1915 Mr Browning was succeeded by Mr Clark Jackson. Considerable technical improvements were introduced over the years and in 1922, when the borough was extended, gas was laid to Briton Ferry. The local works there were closed and the whole of the borough was supplied by the municipal gas undertaking. Its activities were extended, eventually, to the sale of domestic appliances and showrooms were opened in Neath and in the Briton Ferry area of the borough. Bye-products such as tar and coke were produced. New installations were put down in 1935 and a number of reductions in gas prices became a testimony to the efficiency of its undertaking.

The story of the Town's gas had been very similar to that of the water supplies. There had been a long period of private company control, involving much wrangling, followed eventually by the taking over of these utilities by the Corporation. There had, of course, been one difference. The gas supply had been initiated by a recognised local government body, the Parish. Other agencies of local administration must be considered briefly, namely, the Board of Guardians (to which reference had already been made) and the Quarter Sessions.

The Board of Guardians

For a long time the fear had been growing that the cost of Poor Law relief was getting out of hand and that it was encouraging idleness amongst the poor. It was also argued that it encouraged the growth of the birth rate and that the county would not be able to afford to feed a growing population. All of which, of course, was nonsense. The Poor Law Amendment of 1834 was born, mainly out of a simple reluctance to pay the poor rate. Administratively it was more revolutionary than the Municipal Corporation Act, for it carved out the whole county into new divisions called Unions and created new authorities, the Board of Guardians. The latter were elected on a graded property basis the number of votes given to each varying one to twelve according to the value of his property, unlike the simple franchise of the 1835 Act. Also, unlike the Municipal Act which left the corporations largely to control themselves, the new unions were subject to rigid central control.

In order to abolish outdoor relief for able-bodied workers and their families, the Guardians were instructed to set up workhouses which paupers would be compelled to enter and where their lot would be harder than the lowest paid labourer not on relief. The sick and the impotent would continue to be paid relief but the workhouse test would be rigorously applied.

In 1838, the Union workhouse for Neath district was erected at the end of Gnoll Park Road. It was called Lletty Nedd. Neighbouring parishes, forming the union, all contributed to its keep. The conditions inside the workhouse, in its early years were unbelievably bad. In a letter written to the press in December 1838, George Tenant (of the Cadoxton Tenants) describes the building as "that loathsome prison house — that Bastille — the Neath Union". He described the rooms or cells as damp and unventilated. "Stone Vaults", was one of the phrases he used. No fires were possible as there was no hearth or chimney. It became the practice to place a quantity of stone in each cell and the unfortunate inmate was given the task of breaking up the stone in sufficiently small pieces to enable these to pass the two inch mesh grating which was placed in the wall of each cell. The chippings were used for road repairs. The inhuman separation of husband and wife and even parent and child, was a further illustration of how the "sin" of poverty was punished. The "Times" constantly exposed such conditions and Francess Trollope (mother of Anthony Trollope) wrote a novel, "Jesse Phillips", which was a far more violent condemnation of the Victorian workhouse than Dickens' "Oliver Twist". On one occasion, there had been a discussion amongst the Guardians whether to allow beer at Christmas for workhouse inmates. This produced the following satirical lines:

"Go on! Strong drink brought them here
Stop that pint of Christmas beer!"
The paupers reply –
"Oh why do they make all this fuss
Who drinks most, they or us?"

Conditions improved somewhat throughout the century and the workhouse, eventually, closed (except as a Casual Ward) in 1924 when the inmates were moved to Penrhiwtyn (now the General Hospital), all children had by the turn of the century, been transferred to the Bryncoch Cottage Homes where an excellent staff provided very humane care.

In the early years of this century, vagrants including many females, were still numerous enough to cause concern to some of the Guardians. The Neath correspondent of the "Cambrian" reported, on March 1908, that he had, personally, seen many sleeping out in hedges around the Neath district. A circular was sent out by the Bridgend Guardians to each area urging more severe tasks for tramps seeking relief. But the Neath Guardians, obviously of a more humane turn of mind, ignored the suggestion. In 1910, the workhouse matron, Mrs Mills, retired. She was greatly praised by the Guardians, especially for working in such dismal conditions, and with so few facilities.

But the image of the nineteenth century workhouse had embedded itself deeply in the public mind and it took a long time before it was exorcised from the minds of the elderly poor. In 1929, the Poor Law administration came to an end under the 1929 Local Government Act of Mr Neville Chamberlain and responsibility passed to the County Council. The hundred years of Poor Law history has been described as a record of mistaken beliefs frantically adhered to; but there was also much honest and conscientious work by many voluntary and unpaid workers and many successful attempts to humanise the system were made.

The Quarter Sessions

The Local Government Act of 1888, which created the councy councils, brought the long history of the Quarter Sessions to an end. A sharp division was made between the administrative and judicial work of the county. The Sessions retained the judicial side but the administrative business was handed over to the county. We have seen, in a previous chapter, that the Quarter Sessions, beginning as a judicial court in 1542, gradually took over an increasing amount of civil administrative work and became, by the eighteenth century, a major unit of local government in the county, covering a wide spectrum of activities. In addition, it incurred the responsibility for rating in the nineteenth century.

Since 1738, the Sessions had been empowered to levy a rate based on parochial assessments with additional powers granted in 1814. A committee was appointed in 1842 to revise rates (for the purpose of making a general county rate) under the chairmanship of Mr Bichero, a Justice of the Peace. By 1855, assessments had been worked out for every hamlet in Glamorgan. Instead of meeting quarterly, the Quarter Sessions now met every week; such was the pressure of the work involved.

The situation became, eventually, impossible from an administrative point of view and the termination of the civil responsibilities of the Sessions under the 1888 Act was a simple matter of logic. Besides, the whold character of the Quarter Sessions was undemocratic.

The period of Reform from 1835 to 1888 had seen major steps taken in the development of municipal services. A sense of increased civic awareness of the need to extend amenities to cover the needs of the community had shown itself. This had taken place despite periods of stagnation and bitter controversies. Yet there were still many problems to be solved, not only in obtaining further amenities, but also in the field of administrative reform. There was a multiplicity of rate levies. One member of the House, who was urging reform, claimed he had 27 demands, eight from one Parish. In the concluding remarks of his speech, during the debate in 1870 on financial reform, Hugh Goschen (President of the Board of Trade) summed up the position in a few telling words. "The truth, sir, is that we have a chaos as regards authorities, a chaos as regards rates, and worse chaos than all as regards areas."

The next step in Local Government Reform was waiting to be taken and these are to be discussed in Chapter Ten.

CHAPTER 9

Jane Williams (1793-1873) of Aberpergwm and the Cultural Renaissance of the 19th Century

By any standards the most illustrious woman in the history of Neath is Jane Williams. She belonged to the Williams family of Aberpergwm, a family that can trace its lineage back to pre-Norman times in Glamorgan. Neuadd Aberpergwm was a centro of Welsh cultural activities since the Middle Ages. Bardic poetry with its poetic forms of the awdl (ode) and the cywydd (involving the internal rhyme of the cynghanedd) was a feature of Welsh mansions together with singing to the accompaniment of the harp. During the Tudor and Stuart periods bardic activities declined with the anglicisation of the Welsh gentry. The main purpose of the bards in pre-Tudor times was to boost the morale of the Welsh and prophesy that a saviour would arise, and rid them of their English oppressors. With the accession of the Welsh Henry Tudor this era had passed, but at the end of the seventeenth century, a revival of Celtic Studies began and in the eighteenth century it gathered force at Aberpergwm. The revived unrest in Welsh literature was shown in the appointment of Dafydd ap Nicholas to be the domestic bard at the Williams' home.

Culturally speaking Jane Williams was to become the most prominent member of this family. She was taught the harp by Parish Alver and became an outstanding player and also of the mandolin. She was lavishly praised by the English critic Crofton Croker for her beautiful singing. "Nature has given her one of the most exquisite voices I have ever heard — to be compared without disadvantage to Mesdames Sontag and Stockhausen. By no one could the placid airs of Handel and of the great Italian masters be delivered with greater purity and feeling. This was the more rare because her speciality was singing the national songs of Wales to the harp."

But her real claim to fame was the collection and preservation of her Welsh airs and folk-lore. Her collection of fairy tales relating to the Glynneath district was published as a supplement to the book on "Irish

Miss M. Jane Williams of Aber Pergwm (1793-1873), famous collector of original Welsh folk songs and folk tales. One of the leaders of the Celtic Renaissance of the 19th century.

Fairy Legends" and subsequently published in the Handbook to the Vale of Neath (probably by Charles Waring). But it was the publication of, in 1844, of Jane's "Ancient Airs of Gwent and Morganwy" which won for her a first prize at Abergavenny eisteddfod in 1838 for the best collection of Welsh airs. Jane added other airs in 1844 to her collection. In this publication she stated that the songs "are given as she obtained them in their wild and original state among the peasantry of Gwent and Morganwy but especially in Glynneath. No embellishment of the melodies have been made." Among the collection of airs were popular songs such as "Y Bore Glas", "Y Ferch o'r Sger", "Castell Nedd", "Bugeilio Gwenith Gwyn" as well as three airs sung to the lyrics of Dafydd ap Nicholas — "Callan Serchus", "Ffani Blodau Ffair" and "Y Deryn Pur"!

Jane travelled a great deal in her search for material and this before the advent of railways, entailed not a little difficulty. Persuading people to allow her to write down the music of the songs resulted in often humerous situations such as the story of Jane visiting a lonely farmhouse. When the grandmother of the family saw her taking down the music she thought that the black signs were black magic symbols and became very frightened. Magic was very close to people in those days. There is an account of a custom of women dancing in a field on midsummer night in a strange revelry involving a song and ritual of an erotic nature.

The Upper Vale of Neath abounds in fairy stories and legends. Interwoven with these were stories of witchcraft in which Jemima the witch of Blaen Hepste played a prominent part. She had many consultations with John Harris, the celebrated warlock of Cwrt-y-Cadno. Belief in all manner of ghosts and bogies were widespread and the belief is that these were the survivals of ancient deities which were obsessional beliefs amongst the ancient Celts.

Jane moved in a wide circle of cultural friends which included Lady Llanover (wife of Benjamin Hall, Minister of Works, whose name was given to the Westminster Clock, Big Ben). Lady Llanover was a prominent member of the Celtic Renaissance Group. Lady Charlotte Guest was another person involved and was, of course, a translator of the Tales of the Mabinogi. It is now conjectured that Neath Abbey was involved in Welsh Literary history such as the transcription of the famous "Red Book of Hengest".

To Jane Williams posterity must always be grateful for her collecting and preserving the lovely folk songs of Wales — a precious heritage. Aberpergwm House the traditional home of the Williams family since the Middle Ages has alas, met the fate of so many country mansions and is now less than a shell.

The last hundred years have seen a rush of activity of music and other art forms in the town. The great chapel building era at the turn of the century generated a wide field of cultural activities whilst town choirs, opera and operatic societies, orchestras and drama societies added enrichment to community life. Television seems to have had a very minimal effect on such activities. Highlights in our cultural history were the National Eisteddfod held in Neath in 1918 and 1934.

Sir S. T. Evans

Any book on the History of Neath could not omit reference to one of its most distinguished sons in the realm of law and politics. A plaque on the wall of J. G. Brown, Insurance Brokers in New Road, Skewen records the birthplace of Sir S. T. Evans where his parents kept a grocer's shop. He was educated at the Quaker School in Neath Abbey, later at Swansea Collegiate College and Aberystwyth University where he took a degree in Welsh. But later he studied law and became prominent in the Neath Courts. Eventually he entered politics and became an M.P. for Mid-Glamorgan (of which Neath was a part) as a Liberal. In Parliament he embraced many issues such as Temperance, Education, Home Rule and

Tithe Reform. Inevitably he became closely associated with Lloyd George. His legal acumen and brilliant debating powers impressed friends and foes alike in the Commons and he was regarded by some of his friends as a worthy leader of the Liberal Party. His opposition to the South African War matched Lloyd George. He did not neglect local affairs and took a prominent part in establishing the Coedffranc Free Library. He was appointed to the High Office of Solicitor-General in 1908. Two years later however, he left politics when he was offered one of the highest offices in the legal world — that of the Presidency of the Admiralty, Probate and Divorce Division of the High Court. (The extraordinary linking of ships, marriages and wills was to remain until a report of the Evershed Commission in 1953). Utmost dedication to his job produced a massive work on prize law (involving complex cases of contraband goods in wartime etc.) making him the founder and brilliant exponent of modern prize law. He became a G.C.B. in 1916, Hon Doctor of Law in the same year and a Freeman of Swansea and Neath. Lord Birkenhead once remarked that if he had remained in politics he would have become not only Lord Chancellor but a very great one. He died on the eve of the armistice.

CHAPTER 10

The Last Phase (1888-1987)

Neath as the new County Town and the chief seat of the Quarter Sessions — that was the idea which the Borough Council enthusiastically took up when the County of Glamorgan was formed under the 1888 Local Government Act. Every effort was made to get the headquarters of the County and the Sessions established at Neath. It was argued that the town possessed a spacious Town Hall with another larger one almost ready; there was easy access by rail and ample hotel accommodation; and two gaols were also available. It was, alas, of no avail. Accessibility was admitted but it was not conceded that there was adequate accommodation. However, the Inaugural Meeting of the County Council was held in Neath on January 31st 1889 (perhaps, as a consolation prize) in the now completed Gwyn Hall.

This had been built on a site donated by Howel Gwyn, who also made a gift of £200 towards the cost of the building of the hall. The "Squire of Duffryn", as he was called, was the son of William Gwyn, a leading Neath solicitor, who lived in a mansion house opposite Gwyn Hall. Howel was educated at David Davies' excellent school in Queen Street and at Trinity College, Oxford. Almost every conceivable public office had been held by him, including that of Mayor of Neath, Freeman of the Borough, Chairman of the Board of Guardians, High Sheriff of Glamorgan and M.P. for Brecon and also for Falmouth. He built Dyffryn Church, made large gifts towards St Davids' Church and Alderman Davies' School. He died in January, 1888 and his funeral was the public event of the year, despite apalling weather.

The foundation stone of the Gwyn Hall was laid in June, 1887, by Mrs Gwyn, with a great deal of ceremony. The first council meeting was held on the 4th of February, 1889. It had cost £6,000, the contractor being Alderman George, Mayor of the Town in 1897, and the architect, John Norton of London. In the September of 1889, a statute of Howel Gwyn was unveiled by Sir John Llewellyn. The siting of it in the frontage of the Hall, had caused much controversy in the Council as it was thought that this site would "interfere with carriages". An alternative position suggested was opposite St David's Church. History has now re-asserted itself! The choice of a sculptor had also caused much discussion. A press report of May 1888, recorded that Mr Milo Griffiths, the distinguished Welsh sculptor, was in town and had prepared a most artistic model of the late Howel Gwyn for the inspection of the family and of subscribers. It received the highest praise from all concerned, but the sculptor was to be bitterly disappointed, for the order was given to Signor Merrio Raggi, a London artist, who had been responsible for many public statues, including that of Lord Swansea and the Earl of Beaconsfield.

To revert to council matters more directly concerned with public administration, the Reform Act of 1888 was followed, in 1894, by the setting up of urban and Rural District Councils. To complete the reconstruction of Local Government in a democratic sense, it was necessary to give fresh life to the Parish. Included in the Bill, therefore, were popularly elected Parish Councils. Local government was now entirely municipalised, for the principle applied to municipal corporations had now been extended to all other local bodies with the exception of the Board of Guardians. County Boroughs had already been established under the 1888 Act; these were boroughs which had over 50,000 population.

At the same time, Urban and Sanitary Authorities formed under previous Health Acts, were reconstructed and operated in conjunction with the new councils. In practice all this created needless confusion. Instead of consolidating local authority agencies, the proliferation of which had caused such chaos in the past, was, to some extent, perpetuated. Neath Borough Council was to wear several hats for some time to come, Urban Sanitary Authority, Borough Council and even Urban District Council. The latter operated up to 1922. One can only suspect a masochistic urge in our constitutional reformers, and a similar feeling in local councils, considering the way they prolonged this confusion for no apparent reason.

Before the end of the century, a new structural element entered local government. Although ward divisions were permissable under the 1835 Municipal Reform Act, records of electoral returns show that they were not introduced in Neath until 1895. Two wards began to operate in elections in that year, the Melyn or South Ward and the Castle or North Ward. There was a strong argument for the creation of four wards but the over-riding opinion was that this would create "pocket" wards dominated by certain strong personalities, and these would prove just as corrupt as the "pocket" boroughs of the past, as when Neath was "in the pocket" of the Mackworths.

By 1912, another element appeared in local elections. This was party politics, a factor which was destined to play an enormously important part in local government henceforth. Throughout the last century, local issues were not fought on party lines. The conflict was mainly between health reformers and anti-reformers or rate protectionists; although, in many parts of the country, a political element was evident. Whigs and Radicals tended to line up against Tories on issues of economy versus reform. There was, however, no consistency of attitudes in this matter. In Manchester, for instance, the Tories were the "economisers" whilst in Liverpool they were supporters of reformist policies.

At the turn of the century, the Independent Labour Party and Trades Councils and later, the official Labour Party, tended to press for such policies as houses for the workers. Increasing Labour representation tended to coalesce around this issue which made a division between parties on the local plane inevitable. Schools and recreation grounds were issues which became allied to municipal housing.

Representation by the Labour Party on the town council was provided by David Davies, elected in 1901, J. R. Jones, in 1902, and Daniel Harry in 1904. Prominent amongst members of other political persuasions (usually called Independents) were Hopkin Morgan, woollen manufacturer and W. B. Trick, autioneer. Howel Gwyn and J. H. Rowland, who had been dominant in the latter part of the nineteenth century, were now both dead. Another prominent member of the "Independent" category, David Evans-Bevan of Cadoxton House, was surprisingly defeated in the Castle (North) Ward in 1904. Both W. B. Trick and Hopkin Morgan had won seats on the new County Council in 1895.

The council took an unusual step, in 1908, of electing a mayor from outside the corporation. This was Sir Griffith Thomas of Swansea, colliery proprietor and coal exporter. He was also closely associated with the development of Swansea Docks, being a trustee and chairman of the Swansea Harbour Trust. In 1901, he was elected Mayor of Swansea, although (as in Neath) not a member of the Council. His popularity was such that he served as Mayor for three successive years, his mother serving as Mayoress. Sir Griffith celebrated his mayorality in Neath by presenting a new mayoral robe and hat to the Corporation. In 1901, he sold his collieries, which were mainly in the Glynneath and Onllwyn area, to Mr Evans-Bevan of Cadoxton. His home at Cwrt Herbert was a place where many cultural organisations met and enjoyed his hospitality such as various Cymrodorion Societies and the Celtic Congress. Sir Griffith died, a bachelor, in 1922.

The first Labour Mayor in Neath was David Davies, a trade union official with splendid visions of ideal housing estates. He was elected in 1909. Three years later, the second Labour Mayor, Daniel Harry became the town's chief citizen. He was also a trade union official and held office in a remarkable range of political, religious and cultural organisations. Like many of his colleagues at that time, he believed passionately in the value of education. Another prominent labour councillor was J. R. Jones again with stron trade union connections. Councillor Jones was Chairman of the Neath Trades Council for many years. In 1908, he lost his seat on the council probably owing to his lack of support for the fight relating to equality between provided and non-provided schools. He regained it in 1911.

At this time, members of the Council were not circulated with council minutes before meetings and there was growing dissatisfaction over this. In January 1913, it was proposed that this be done as most councils had already been operating this practice, as had the Neath Board of Guardians. The motion, however, was lost as the majority of the 'older' members felt that printing and circulating minutes would be too great an expence on the rates. Efficiency was thus again sacrificed on a "rate protection" argument; this time for the very modest annual sum of £120. Minutes were not in fact, circulated until 1922 and reports were not included until after the last war. Members had to be content with officers' reports being read to them by the Town Clerk, at each particular meeting.

The election of councillors was not the only one which took place. The 1835 Act provided for the election of auditors. It was noticeable that the number of electors turning out for these events was, not surprisingly, very much smaller than for the council elections. In 1911, for instance, two auditors were elected (from three candidates) with 157 and 147 votes compared with the average vote of about 600 for councillors.

These were rumbustious times in the sphere of local policies. The "hustings" meetings at which all candidates were expected on the platform to say their piece, were a feature of all elections. Any candidate who failed to appear could expect very short shrift from the electorate. These events were no places for public representatives with sensitive feelings, being often a "Roman holiday" for hecklers. On the other hand, they provided opportunities for candidates with wit and intelligence to show their mettle. "Hustings" continued to be held in Neath well into the 1930's although in the Parliamentary Election of 1945, a meeting of this kind was held in the Gwyn Hall. On one occasion following a change of party by one councillor in 1913, a number of townspeople marched in the mayoral procession with their coats turned inside out.

The uninhibited reaction of some sections of the public to local politicians could also be seen in the satirical posters of the 1870's. Then came the more libellous publications of that wayward eccentric, C. R. Trueman. He was a photographer by trade and lived in a house on the corner of Penrhiwtyn Street. During the period 1900-1929, he was an arch-baiter of the Council producing post-cards for sale with caricatures of local councillors with "Quill" which contained all manner of scurrilous accusations particularly against one prominent member of the authority and the Chief Constable. One of the very much milder accusations was that the Mayor and some of his colleagues drank after house with the connivance of the police, but in order to evade the law, they placed a bottle of H.P. Sauce on the table! Trueman served numerous prison sentences for libel and slander; but he certainly, was a colourful character in the town with his top hat and frock coat. He was often seen in mayoral processions carrying a model of a gas meter with a placard containing dark hints of councillors enjoying free gas. Sometimes, he was seen carrying a coffin with even more sinister innuendos. The police, apparently, were asked to arrest him for obstruction if he was caught standing around: so he employed two dodges which he claimed made him immune from arrest. He either walked with one foot in the gutter and one on the pavement, which, he argued, made him legally immune from any charge of obstructing the highway or he just kept moving without stopping for change whilst selling his "literature".

Mr Ernest Richards told me that he worked for Trueman when a boy in his photographic business and remembers him at lunch in his room (which was littered with all kinds of paraphernalia) enjoying his customary meal of bread and cheese and a pint of milk. He always placed the cheese on the floor. Suddenly, he would bring his foot down sharply and, almost with a sleight of hand, Trueman would be waving a dead mouse before the fascinated stare of his assistant! One of the latter's jobs would be to fetch a massive law book from another room whenever his employer required to prepare his case before appearing in court, where he always conducted his own defence and always lost.

Before he came to Neath he appeared to have lived in Shropshire for, in the Assize Court there in 1889, he was plaintiff in a case of slander by a Mr Deakin. The latter had accused Trueman of many improper acts including the taking of obscene photographs. Judgement was given to defendant, Deakin. There was a general belief in Neath that Trueman was a solicitor's clerk dismissed from some local council! He seemed to have been aware of his weakness for he described himself, in "Quill", as a monomaniac.

Gradually, the percentage of Labour representatives on the Town Council, and in 1932, majority control was established on a 13-11 basis. In 1934, J. E. Emmanuel, the first mayor of the new extended Borough, was elected for the South Ward. In the realm of County representation, George Gethin, of the Briton Ferry Ward, became the first Labour representative in 1925 and the Rev. Degwel Thomas (South Ward), in 1928. The latter, in 1931, unseated a member of the "old establishment" in the person of Theodore Gibbins, Quaker industrialist of the Melyn and Briton Ferry Tinplate Works.

When normal council work was resumed after the war, a new factor entered local politics with the formation of the Citizen's Guild and Ratepayer's Association. Opposition to the Labour Party was now on a more organised basis.

Neath and the Spanish Civil War

The Civil War in Spain (1936-39) was, of course, a prelude to the Second World War. Beginning as a domestic crisis (born of the economic depression) it quickly assumed vastly significant international implications and became a catalyst of the political upheavals of the times.

Neath was in the forefront of towns that reacted to the challenge of fascism by its participation in the International Brigade, its activities on the home front ("Aid to Spain") and its hospitality to the Basque children who were evacuated from Spain. Neath men who lost their lives in the Civil War were Harold Davies, A. Skinner, V. Estaban, J. Strangward, F. Zamora. Alfred Evans, Ivor Davies and D. Peters were taken prisoner (a full account can be read in "Neath and the Spanish Civil War" by the writer of these pages).

Women in Local Government

Typical of the age-old male prejudice against women, the only duties allocated to them in the parishes and manors of the seventeenth and eighteenth centuries were inferior and onerous tasks. Not for them were the offices of churchwardens, Portreeve or Recorder or even of minor offices.

It was not until the Poor Law Amendment Act of 1834 that women could vote and serve on the Board of Guardians: at least it was so in theory. In practice, women could not vote because they could not legally own property until 1870 and, therefore, could not be ratepayers. Under the 1835 Act, the status of burgess earned the right to vote but remained exclusively male until 1870. The end of this exclusiveness was due partly, to a movement commenced by John Stuart Mill by his presentation in the Commons of a petition of 1,499 signatures praying that all householders should be enfranchised regardless of sex.

Yet prejudice persisted and in February 1888, a letter appeared in the Swansea "Cambrian" from a London lady, Caroline Biggs, urging that women should be represented on the Board of Guardians. She pointed out that not a single woman was appointed to serve on any Board in the whole of Wales.

It was in 1907, that it was enacted that women could not only vote but also, be elected on Borough or County Councils on the same terms as men. It was surely, one of the more ludicrous anomilies in the history of the franchise that women could serve as councillors, aldermen and, presumably, mayors at a time when they were considered unfit to vote in Parliamentary elections. How peculiar, also, was the fact that, although women had this right to vote and be elected on councils, no woman was ever standing for election; and this was at a time when some women were campaigning vigorously, and often suffering grivously in the process, for the Parliamentary franchise.

In the years up to 1914, the Suffragette movement was in full swing. Both in Neath and neighbouring towns, many meetings were held. National figures such as Mrs Corbett Ashley addressed meetings in the Albert Hall, many stormy scenes occurring there.

In 1910, a meeting was held in the Melyn School. It was reported that a crowd of children followed a group of yound women who were distributing propaganda leaflets after the meeting, and pelted them with every kind of missile. Hostility was not always encountered, but to deal with the complex motivations relating to the Suffragette Cause is hardly relevant to the subject of this book. In the Neath district a branch of the Union of Woman Suffrage Societies operated. The secretary was Mrs W. G. Tonna and the President Mrs Dorothy Coombe-Tennant, who was also a prominent member of the Peace Society. The branch met in the Mikado Cafe but open air meetings were frequently held, speakers (some were men) addressing the crowd from a dog-cart. In Glynneath, at a meeting held in Bethania Chapel, a voice from the gallery demanded of the women speakers, "Would you defend your country at time of war?" The reply from the platform (or pulpit) was, "It was women who repelled the French invasion at Fishguard!"

It was not until 1922 that women were represented on the Neath Borough Council, four years after the first woman M.P. was elected to Parliament in the person of the Countess Marchievicx, the Irish Republican (the Countess, in prison for her rebellious acts against the British parliament, never actually took her seat). The first woman councillor in Neath was Mrs Lilian Evans, wife of Dr John Evans but, after serving for three years representing the North Ward, she lost her seat to John Morris in the 1925 election. Thirteen years were to elapse before another woman candidate, Miss Katie Davies (also an Independent) was to serve on the Borough Council. Miss Davies defeated Frederick Loader by nine votes.

She represented the South Ward until 1947, when Gilbert Rosser and W. E. Watkins won two seats for the Labour Party.

It was Briton Ferry which provided the next woman councillor; she was Mrs Hilda Howells returned unopposed in 1952 and again in 1954, together with a new entrant into local government, Mrs Mary Moule. Mrs Howells became the first woman Mayor in 1964 and Mrs Moule the second woman to be elected mayor two years later. In 1986, Councillor Iris Hobbs became the third woman to be elected Mayor. Miss M. Lewis (1976) and Mrs R. Matthews (1987) are also members of the Council.

The Extension of the Borough

The boundaries of the Borough remained remarkably similar (in their main features) throughout the earlier centuries. Various piece-meal extensions had been made in the eighteenth, nineteenth and twentieth centuries. The largest and most significant extension took place in 1922 when the area administered by the Briton Ferry Urban District Council was amalgamated with the Neath Borough. A proposed extension of the Borough was mentioned as early as 1833 in the Report of Commissioners for Municipal Reform.

Between 1919 and 1921, Neath Borough, Neath Rural District and Swansea Town authorities were engaged in discussions about boundary extensions. Swansea required Coedfranc (and parts of the parishes of Blaenhonddan and Duffryn Clydach). Neath applied for the inclusion of Briton Ferry, Baglan, Lower Blaenhonddan, Coedfranc and the parishes of Dulais Lower and Llantwit Lower. The attitude of the Neath Rural District Council was expressed in a letter sent to the Borough Council in November 1921, in which they made it clear that they would not agree to parts of the Rural area being joined to the Borough, but the extremely interesting view was expressed that a total amalgamation of the whole of the Rural District with Neath would be desirable; the whole or nothing. This was, of course, exactly what local government reorganisation brought about fifty years later! However, the Neath Council considered that the upper parts of the valleys were too rural in character for an urban authority and did not support the proposal. What differences in the subsequent history of this area would have occurred if the amalgamation had taken place in 1921, is one of the "ifs" of history.

A local enquiry was set up in February 1921 by the Ministry (sitting in Swansea) to consider the various claims and counter claims made by the various authorities. The main decision made was the splitting up of Coedfranc between Neath and Swansea. This was a very artificial division which satisfied neither authority and it was set aside by a Commons Committee in July 1922. It, however, confirmed Neath's claim to Briton Ferry and Llantwit Lower and, in a later agreement with Port Talbot, the town acquired an elongated area embracing the river mouth. Briton Ferry thus became part of the Borough of Neath but it possessed a very strong identity of its own and this has, largely, been retained even today.

Municipal Transport – The Horse and Gas Trams

The story of Transport in the Borough follows the same pattern as that of water and gas, namely, a development from private undertaking to municipal ownership.

The earliest utility in the transport category was introduced into Liverpool in 1868, followed by three tramways, being introduced into London. The formation of the Neath and District Tramway company in 1873 was, therefore, a comparatively early venture. In 1875, a horse-drawn tramway began to operate between Skewen and Briton Ferry. Again the similarity to gas and water stories became emphasised when the tramway company ran into financial difficulties. Main roads were taken over by the County Council from the Highways Board in 1888 and, almost immediately, there was trouble over the conditions of the track. The Government favoured municipal ownership of tramways provided private companies did the work of the actual running of them, but eventually, this attitude changed and local authorities were allowed to run their own tramways. By 1896, the Neath undertaking got into increased financial difficulties and was eventually bought by the Corporation for £40,000. A prominent member of the Tram Company was Councillor Richard Bartlett who was involved in many enterprises in the town. Eventually, he bought out the other members of the company basing his venture on the probability of the tolls, which had been a heavy financial liability, being terminated very soon. But insolvency took over his company before the burden of tolls was able to be shed. He, therefore, sold out to the Corporation. It is not clear whether he also took over a horse-bus company which had been operating in competition with the trams. It is highly probable that this competition and excessive tolls were responsible for the financial troubles of the tram company. By 1890, all tolls were abolished and the press reported that the trams were now to cost the same as the horse buses namely two pence from Neath to Briton Ferry instead of three pence; in the past they had always paid a higher toll than the horse buses.

The Neath Tramways Act of 1897 enabled the Council to work the Tramways by mechanical power if they so wished. (The horse bus service had terminated). The motor car was in its infancy. An amusing incident in the Council Chamber was reported on August 10th 1899, when the passing

of a "newly arrived car, flitting gaily past the Chamber, brought the whole council rushing to the windows to gaze at this new wonder."

In October 1896, the Council was informed that trams driven by gas-power were operating in Lytham St Annes and a visit there was immediately arranged. A very good impression must have been made, for in the very next year, gas trams began to run in Neath. The service operated very successfully except whilst negotiating Skewen Hill where the passengers often had to supply extra power by pushing. By 1914, however, the tramways appeared as an obsolete service, but the useful service it was able to perform in conveying workers to factories during the war years, prolonged its life. Eventually, on July 30th 1920, the service came, finally, to an end. The discovery of the main body of a gas tram (used as a garden shed) in the garden of Mrs Beddoes of Gardners' Lane, by members of the Neath Antiquarian Society, led to its purchase by the Neath Borough Council. It is being expertly refurbished by the Neath Borough Training Agency. The Neath Gas Tram service, when it came to its end in 1923, was

This was the last gas tram to operate in the world and it has been skilfully renovated by the trainees of the Borough Training Agency working under competent supervision. *(By permission of Mr Sylwyn Lawrence, the Agency's Co-ordinator).*

the oldest in the world, and what is now a showpiece in the Agency's workshops is the oldest existing tram in the world.

The substantial unemployment in the post-war years resulted in many appeals to the Council for work for those seeking employment and the taking up of the tramway tracks was one of the many jobs allocated to the unemployed. Road works on a rota system was a regular feature of Council policy for many years during the depression, and in 1922, £4,000 was allocated for the widening of Old Road.

Omnibuses now took over public transport. For a time, the council toyed with the idea of a municipal bus service, but finally, decided to leave it to private enterprise. A part of Victoria Gardens was taken over and a bus centre established.

Neath Gas Tram. (By permission of the Neath Antiquarian Society).

Libraries

As with the other services dealt with, the Library service began by private organisations and individual enthusiasms. The early councils had certainly little to boast of in the way of initiative.

The first Library which appeared in Neath, was due to the Philosophical and Antiquarian Society which was founded in 1834, a year earlier than the birth of the Royal Institution in Swansea. It was enormously successful in its early years and showed every promise of permanence. Housed at first in the Mackworth Great House (the site of the Mackworth Hotel demolished in 1937), it later acquired premises in Queen Street. A collection of books and prints was donated from a wide circle of members. Gifts of money included £100 from H. J. Grant and £5 from Howel Gwyn. The Library was meticulously run with a formidable list of fines for breaches of rules. As well as a library, there was also a museum established which had cases well filled with a variety of exhibits. The curator of the museum was John Grainger (of the Neath ship repairing firm) with Charles Waring (author of "Handbook of the Vale of Neath") taking over in 1852. The society undertook restoration work at Neath Abbey in 1848 of which the Rector of Neath, the Rev. H. Knight, was the driving force. A keen interest in astronomy by some members led to the idea of building an observatory on the same premises in Queen Street. A telescope was purchased and a tower was built but funds did not permit the expense of the mounting of the instrument.

The rest of the story of the Society is a sad one. Old members left, some died and there were very few new recruits. It finally closed down in 1860. The Society decided to return exhibits to the owners and books were auctioned realising £100. There was never any question about the Corporation taking over; at that time it could not even make up its mind about supplying water and sanitary facilities let alone lending its support to what amounted to the first Arts Centre to be established in Wales.

The Mechanic's Institute and Alfred Russel Wallace

Long before state-aided education became established the deep hunger for learning amongst the people made itself known in various ways. One of these was the formation of Mechanic's Institutes, which was an attempt to provide mechanics and other workers with elementary and technical instruction

In October 1843, such an Institute was formed in Neath and one of the teachers was a young man named Alfred Russel Wallace destined to become a world famous figure in natural science enjoying an equal status with Charles Darwin. Wallace had come to Neath in 1841 when he was 18

Alfred Russel Wallace, aged 25 in 1848, destined to become a world-famous biologist.

years old, accompanied by his elder brother William. He was born in Usk and when his family moved to Hertfordshire he attended a private school until the age of 15. Eventually he moved to London with his brother and there became qualified surveyors after attending evening classes. The two brothers came to Neath to work and were employed to work and survey the Parish of Cadoxton. He stayed at Bryncoch Farm and later on in Llantwit Cottage. During his spare time he spent long hours in the Vale of Neath studying plant life. He was fascinated with the profound mysteries that lay behind the rich diversity of the fauna and flora of the Neath Valley. What explanation could he make for the variety of species and what was the origin of the fantastic diversity of such species? In his autobiography Wallace described his years in Neath as the most formative years of his life.

At first the Mechanic's Institute was held in the Town Hall. Here Wallace became a teacher in Geology and Astronomy and more elementary lessons in Arithmetic and English. Soon it was felt that a larger building was necessary and Wallace was the successful designer of such a building in Church Place. It was completed in 1847. The library expanded as did the range of subjects taught. Wallace commenced classes in heat, optics and hydrostatics illustrating his astonishing versatility. But the Institute did not prosper. Long working hours made it difficult for young men to attend and the autocratic attitude of the management, composed of the 'elite' of the town, was also a factor. In 1898, the Institute closed and the Corporation established a free Public Library there with a Mr John Morgan as Librarian.

Reverting to the story of Alfred Wallace; it was soon after the opening of the Mechanics Institute that he left for the Amazon with a friend in order to pursue his absorbing interest in natural life. He was influenced in his decision by a book by W. H. Edwards "A Voyage up the Amazon" in which a bewildering variety of plants and insects was described. He was to spend four years in the Amazon area collecting specimens of all kinds. On his return journey a fire on board ship disastrously destroyed much of his collection.

Mechanics Institution, Church Place, Neath, now to be transformed into a Borough Museum.

Looking for new worlds to explore and to continue his studies he left for Malaya in 1852. There he was to develop his theory of Natural Selection. He wrote to Charles Darwin informing him of his theory and this astonished Darwin who had also formulated the same theory. It was agreed that they would present a joint paper on the subject. This was not a discovery of the theory of evolution which had been around for some time but a description of the mechanism by which evolution had come about. Darwin was to publish in the next year his epoch making book on "The Origin of Species" which finally established the theory of evolution in scientific circles but which aroused intense opposition especially in the religious world.

Wallace was to develop much wider interests than Darwin in later life. He had always been an avid reader in many subjects from an early age. He was now to develop a keen interest in social and economic problems such as land reform, and ecology, pacifism and spiritualism. These later interests earned him much ridicule from Huxley who also hostile to Wallace's theory of a Directive Intelligence being a factor in evolution.

In his later years he was to visit with his wife the Vale of Neath which he loved, and an amusing story is recounted in his autobiography. On meeting a road worker in Pontneddfechan, he asked him whether he felt proud to live in such a beautiful place. The man replied, "I would rather be back home in Lincolnshire. This place is nothing but hills and stones."

The Mechanics' Institute has now been splendidly renovated and a Borough Museum is being developed. It promises to be a major cultural asset to the Borough.

As far as the State was concerned, the first Public Libraries Act was passed in 1855, the result of an exhaustive report by William Ewart, M.P. for Dumfries on information supplied to him by a young Welshman, on the Staff of the British Museum, by the name of Edward Edwards. He, later, became the first librarian of the Manchester Public Library. Edwards had seen that towns, on the continent had forged ahead in the establishment of free Public Libraries. The 1855 Act was an extremely grudging statute limiting the rate of a half-penny in the pound and giving no power to spend money on books. These, presumably, had to be donated or produced out of a conjuror's hat. But, later, more rational Acts followed and, in May 1897, the Public Libraries Act was adopted by Neath Corporation. At first, the lease of the old Mechanics' Institute was taken over for the establishment of a library. A valuabe collection of books by Miss Mayzod Rowlands, daughter of Alderman J. H. Rowlands, the Mayor of Neath, provided a valuable foundation. A disastrous fire, however, destroyed the majority of its books in January, 1905.

The Council decided to build a new library in Victoria Gardens Road at a cost of £3,646, £2,000 of which had been left in the will of Miss Rowlands towards a new building. £100 was donated by David Evans-Bevan and the foundation stone was laid by the Mayoress, Mrs Evans-Bevan on October 20th 1904. In September 1905, the Library was formerly opened by the Mayor, David Evans-Bevan during his third term of Office. In his speech at the opening ceremony, he alluded to his departure from Council work owing to his defeat in the recent Election.

Two years earlier, the Briton Ferry Library had been built on land given by the Earl of Jersey together with a gift of £500. It was this building that housed the Council Chamber of the new Briton Ferry Urban District Council which had been formed in 1894. The early librarians of these libraries were without specialised training but they were persons of natural ability and with a great love of books.

Financial restrictions by the Exchequer persisted and, in 1920, we find the library committee protesting at the limitation to a penny rate for library expenditure. This centralised control disappeared under the 1929 Local Government Act.

The Library contained many excellent prints and paintings, the most valuable being a work by Benjamin West entitled "Abraham and Isaac" (now removed to the Civic Centre). A press report in May 1910 refers to the presentation of this painting to the Neath Borough Council by Mr Joseph Rombach of the Cambrian Arms Hotel, Melyn.

A somewhat bizarre background story was recounted, as follows. "The painting once belonged to an eccentric gentleman who purchased it in Belgium and took it with him on extensive sea voyages. Going ashore in some foreign capital, he disappeared and never returned to the ship. The Captain of the ship, seeing this huge, dirty canvas regarded it as unlucky and had it stored in Swansea. It was sold, later, to pay for storage costs. The painting was bought by a relative of Mr Rombach to whom it was presented. Mr Rombach found it too large to hang in his own house, so he presented it to the Neath Council for hanging in the Gwyn Hall. However, the Librarian Mr George, wished to have it in the Library. This was two years ago in 1908. The painting was dirty and obscure but two figures could be clearly seen. The Library Committee decided to have it cleaned and a picture of rare beauty was revealed with the artists' signature, no less than Benjamin West's, in the lower left hand corner. West (1738-1820) was born in Pennsylvania of Quaker Stock. He became a favourite of George III and a President of the Royal Academy".

The Library Committee of February 1911 record the fact that the picture was, on expert advice, insured for £1,000, an appreciable sum in those days. It also records a gift by Mrs Rombach of a print of a portrait of Benjamin West, which it was decided to hang in the Library.

The works of West, although of considerable merit, are not of course considered to be in the "top flight" category. He was referred to by many of his contemporaries as the "American Raphael", an obviously absurd exaggeration. It is of interest to note that a psycho-analytical comment by Mr Merlin Thomas (of Gnoll Park Road, Neath), attracted praise from Dr Geraldine Krag, an Americans psychologist who passed it on to Professor Von Erffa of the University of New Jersey whilst the latter was engaged in writing a biography of West.

The Librarian's Reports contain some very frank views on public tastes. In 1906, we find him reporting that, to his displeasure, young people were demanding more fiction on the shelves and there was a constant complaint generally, that the works of Marie Correlli were not on the shelves. On December 30th 1911, he included in his report the following delicious passage. "In my humble opinion the remedy for the restlessness of the day in the industrial world is the cultivation of a more enlightened mind amongst the working classes. You have in the library a fine collection of books on economics. This would silence the rash and foolish utterances of not only the workers but also of those who presume to be their leaders." One can safely assume that the Library was not stocked with the works of Marx and Engels or even Robert Blackford's "Merrie England", Henry George's "Taxation of Land Values" and Robert Tressell's "The Ragged Trousers Philanthropist", books which were avidly read by many of the workers in those days. The recent reprinting of Tressell's book indicates that interest in such books still is very much alive. A children's Library has been added to Neath's Central Library and this is now greatly used.

W.E.A. classes and local debating societies were well attended and, in a meeting of the Library committee in January 1920, permission was sought and given for a class for miners to be held weekly in the Lecture Room which would be paid for by the education authority.

Many lectures took place in the Library and there were well patronised men and women's reading rooms and also, a reference room. The times of opening were 10.30 to 12, 3 to 4, and 6.30 to 8.00 p.m. On Saturday, the evening session was extended to 9 p.m. It would be interesting to know the reaction of the staff and public today to these times of opening. Those were days of course, when owing to long working hours many were not free until late in the evening. It was a time when most shops were open on Saturdays until 11 p.m.

The Library service developed steadily and the number and variety of books extended. During the long depression of the inter-war years there was a big increase in the issue of non-fiction books especially those dealing with the reconstruction of the social and economic order.

Dorothy Tennant (Lady Stanley) daughter of Charles Tennant, became a distinguished painter in oils and an artist in 'black and white'.

Reading and arguing about the shape of the "New Jerusalem" alleviated many hours of boredom and misery whilst "on the dole".

In 1927, Lady Stanley presented a splendid collection of paintings of Old Briton Ferry by the celebrated Thomas Horner, to the Neath Antiquarian Society. These valuable art treasures now hang in the Civic Centre.

Education

The shadows of the French Revolution were still darkening people's minds in the early part of the nineteenth century and the governing classes were frightened at the idea of mass education because it might lead to social unrest. There was also a much deeper, more entrenched belief, that the social class structure was divinely ordained.

In the Commons, in 1807 a member (Mr Gibby) crystallised this attitude in a speech protesting against the education of pauper children which he claimed "would be found to be prejudicial to the morals and happiness of the working classes; it would encourage them to despise their lot in life instead of making them good servants in agriculture and other laborious employments to which their rank in society had destined them; instead of teaching them subordination, it would render them fractivious and refractory; it would enable them to read seditious pamphlets, vicious books and publications against Christianity; it would render them insolent to their superiors". Hannah Moore, a pioneer in the provision of Sunday Schools for children, was to write that "to teach the poor to read without providing them with safe books has always appeared to me to be a dangerous method". To this lady religion was the enemy for this encouraged revolt against authority whether human or divine. The Bishop of London went further for, in 1803, he was expressing the view that "it is safest for both the government and the religion of this country to let the lower classes remain in the state of ignorance in which nature has placed them".

But other and more enlightened forces were at work and, in 1833, the first State aid to education was granted. This was a sum of £20,000 for erecting school buildings, this to go to two voluntary agencies, the National Society (Anglican) and the British Society (undenominational). In the same year, the Government made a grant of £50,000 for the royal stables which made sure that it kept its sense of proportion! Further advances were, however, made in 1856 with the creation of an Education Department and, in 1861, when a system of grants were made on the basis of a payment by results which on purely educational grounds, was to be severely criticised. It was not until 1870 that a system of universal, compulsory education was introduced. Voluntary schools were allowed to continue but school Boards were set up to fill the gaps. By 1876, there were sufficient schools, it was thought, to enforce compulsory education.

But, before this, was a long history of charity and private schools, which could provide for a special study in itself. We can, therefore, make a brief selective survey only, as our concern is with education as a local authority serice. One category of such schools was that set up by industrialists for the children of their workers. The first of these was the Melyn Works School established by Sir Humphrey Mackworth in 1694 and which lasted until 1720. Later schools in Neath Abbey, Aberdulais, and Cwmgwrach opened. The school at the Abbey was built by the ironworks proprietor, Tregelles Price, the one at Aberdulais by the tinplate firm of W. Llewellyn and Sons and the Cwmgwrach School by the ironworks owner, W. Jevons.

The Education Report of 1847, despite the fact that it was severely criticised for its lack of sympathy and understanding of the Welsh, does provide some factual details of conditions in these works schools. The Aberdulais building was a dismal place with nothing but a few worn, dirty cards hanging on the wall providing illustrative material and a copy of the rules and regulations of the Aberdulais Brass Band above the fireplace. The School at Neath Abbey seemed a better place, with books and stationery provided. For the boys, there was an attempt to integrate their studies with the iron works and the girls with nursery activities. A system of stoppages from wages (one penny per week) was organised which helped to run the school.

The private schools varied from small "Dame Schools" to boarding schools. There were a dozen schools catering for the poorer children: these were situated in the Green, Queen Street, James Street, Eastgate Street, Water Street and Wind Street. Schools described as "above the use of the poor" were for the most part situated in Queen Street. Here there were schools run by Miss Price and Miss Andrews, where the fees in both were ten shillings per quarter; the Rev. J. Jeffreys (a Neath Curate) where the pupils paid three shillings and sixpence and upwards; Mr Thoms' Boarding School with fees of 25 guineas per annum (25 boarders and 8 day pupils were on roll). In Water Street, there was a school under Miss Bannister where 15 pupils paid seven shillings per quarter. In Green Street was the chief private school (the "Academy") administered by David Davies. The fees here were ten shillings and sixpence upwards and there were 35 pupils on roll. This was where all the well-to-do pupils went.

It was, however, about Sunday Schools that the Report had the most significant things to say. These were described "as exhibiting the most characteristic developments of native intellect and the efforts of the mass of people to educate themselves upon their own model. These schools have been almost the sole and most congenial centres of education. Through their agency the younger portion of the adult labouring classes in Wales read the scriptures in their mother tongue. One fifth of the entire population attended these schools. Sunday to the Welshman is more than a day of devotion and bodily rest. It is the last chance of the week of showing himself in his own character. He shows his sense of it by a suit of clothes hardly less Sabbatical than the day itself. I do not remember seeing anyone in rags in a single Sunday School even in the poorer districts. They always seem to be better dressed on Sunday than the same classes in England. This original idea of the Welsh Sunday School (a mixture of worship, discussion and elementary instruction which the congregation performs and without any other agency than its own) is found under every variety of development".

The Commissioners were often extremely unfair in their remarks (their Report was called "The Treason of the Blue Books" by the Welsh) but

Sunday Schools were evidently recognised as highly significant and important to the people in Wales. Sunday observances generally enabled them to be liberated from the drudgery and oppression of the rest of the week. Zoar seemed to have been the headquarters of the Sunday Schools Movement and here meetings of all the neighbouring schools were held every three months, when prizes for various achievements were distributed. The tradition of Sunday Schools was of course, established by Thomas Charles and Griffith Jones in the eighteenth century. These were known as Circulating Schools and several were established in the Neath District. Some of the local gentry considered it an obligation of their class to help schools in various ways from the payment of the weekly contributions to bestowing special treats. Unfortunately gestures of this kind appeared too often as patronising the poor for which the latter were expected to be eternally grateful. A Sunday School treat by the Penrose Family produced the following in the local press.

Scenes such as these our beings raise
Scenes such as these demand our praise
We love and respect those all the more
Who stoop to please the neighbouring poor.

Schools opened by the National Society and the British and Foreign Society were in some measure, probably the result of the 1847 Report. One British School was established near Orchard Place Chapel, in 1856. This was, eventually, transferred to the Gnoll. A church school (Alderman Davies) was opened in 1858 from the money accruing out of £200 left in 1719 by a former Portreeve of the town, Alderman John Davies. The purpose of this bequest was to erect a school for the "twenty of ye Poorer Sort of ye Inhabitants". A small part of this charity had been used to set up the Merra School in Victoria Gardens in 1813. It was, incidentally, at the dinner following the opening ceremony of Alderman Davies' School, that a marathon speech-making session took place. No fewer than 25 toasts were spoken to. The press reporter confessed that he fell asleep long before they terminated.

The Western University of Great Britain

The most exciting educational project initiated in Wales in the mid-nineteenth century was the proposed Science University at the magnificently sited Gnoll House, in Neath. But although preparations of the most advanced kind were made, the idea never materialised. If it had, the character of the subsequent history of the town would have been substantially different and it would have been Neath rather than Swansea which would have today a University of 3,500 students.

Why did it fail? Before this question is answered let us look briefly at the elaborate plans which were made for its establishment which Iolo Wyn Williams has unearthed (*vide* Collegiate Faculty of Education Swansea, 1966). In the May of 1857, a 90 page Prospectus was published. The college was described as a "National Institution adapted to the wants of the Age" and the object was "To complete the Education of Gentlemen above the age of 16 in the practical application of science to the Management of Manufacture, Land, Commerce, the Public Services, the Professions and other pursuits". It was clear that the venture was inspired by the example of continental countries which had been influenced by our own Great Exhibition of 1851. The College would function independently under the name of the "Western University of Great Britain".

Seven Professors were appointed, all of whom had distinguished academic backgrounds. They were T. Spencer Cobbold (Natural History), The Rev. Andrew Wilson (Human History), E. H. Wehnert (Design), The Rev. C. Woollaston (Mechanics), J. E. Rogers (Chemistry), the Rev. Bath Powers (Physics), and Arthur Cayley (Mathematics). The latter was the foremost mathematician of his time and the author of nearly a thousand original mathematical papers. Professor Wehnert was, incidentally, responsible for illustrations in such classics as "Pilgrim's Progress", Anderson's "Fairy Tales" and "Robinson Crusoe". There were also, resident tutors and assistant lecturers to complete the staffing. The Professors were to be paid £500 compared to an average of £300 at Oxford.

Plans were made for elaborate residential quarters for the students and the University was to be equipped with an observatory, and a farm museum in addition to the normal requirements. The curriculum was set out in detail and several projects were outlined. Many were concerned with the utilisation of waste products. One of these was concerned with an estimated £12,000 worth of sulphur thrown away every month through the chimneys of the copper works in the Swansea district. If such a project had been successfully pursued what environmental devastation might have been avoided! It was, also, suggested that the University would take over the local Parish Roads as an exercise in the study of road building and road maintenance.

The reasons given for choosing Neath were that the town was equidistant from the West Coast of Ireland, the North Coast of Scotland, and the East and South Coast of England; that it was within six hours rail from London, although the students would be of sufficient distance from the temptations and allurements of large cities; that it was within access of mines (coal and iron), lead copper, tin and silver, limestone, docks etc. In addition, the estate had 1,000 acres of arable land, 300 of woodland and 100 of marsh.

The Gnoll Prospectus was signed by the three members of the Executive Council. One of these was none other than Bullock Webster, Steward of the Gnoll Estates whom we have mentioned with regard to the story of Neath's Water Supply. In 1857, Henry John Grant was living on his Hertfordshire estate and had leased the Gnoll Estate to Webster for seven years. The other two were L. C. Hertslet, Librarian at the Foreign Office and Trelawney Saunders, a prominent member of the Geographical Society. Fifty six of the local gentry signed their support.

However, on November 13th, the "Cambrian" regretfully reported that the "Gnoll College had gone to the abyss where all failures of abortive schemes lie in dull oblivion . . . nobody can deny but that the nation required it, but Neath has refused the honour offered her".

But the "Cambrian" was always a little too ready to castigate the Borough Council for there were many reasons for the failure of this well-intentioned project. In the first place the fees were too high. One hundred guineas to enter and 200 guineas a year were unrealistic to say the least, especially as the Paris Ecole Centrale, upon which the Gnoll University was modelled, charged only £37. To plan for 200 students in the first year was, therefore, inviting failure. There was no attempt to consider local Welsh interests. Another deciding factor was the defection of Webster who had always lived precariously as regards finances. He found himself £4,000 in debt and, eventually, spent some time in prison. We do not know whether any students actually arrived in Neath but it is recorded that the Rev. Bath Power, Professor of Physics, certainly reached the town for he preached two very excellent sermons in the Parish Church on Sunday, November 8th. What a pity they were not recorded as surely he must have made reference to the proposed University. The books of the College's bankers, Messrs Jones, Lloyd an important private banking house, would have indicated any nomination fees paid but such records have, seemingly, not survived.

If the Gnoll University had been established, it would have been in very exclusive company as, of present universities, only Oxford, Cambridge, University College and King's College London, Durham, Owen's College, Manchester and Lampeter were in existence. Lampeter, at that time, had not, of course, acquired university status although it could grant the degree of B.D.

Another 'might have been' page in the history of the Gnoll House occurred in 1926 when a plan for adapting the building for a Girls Grammar School was planned. A detailed plan, fully costed, was drawn up but it never materialised.

So of the three educational projects with a leaning to scientific learning, the Mechanic's Institute and the Scientific and Philosophical Society, were established and flourished for a time but, eventually, ended their existence. The most ambitious of them, the Gnoll University, was one which incorporated many brilliant ideas relevant to the needs of the industrial age (some of which we are today only beginning to cope with) but fundamental errors had been made and the Institution was, alas stillborn.

The School Boards were responsible for erecting four schools before the Boards' abolition under the 1902 Act. They were Neath Road in 1876, Vernon Place in 1894, Herbert Road in 1898 and the Gnoll Schools in 1899. To operate compulsory attendence, officers were appointed who became known as "Whippers-in" or "Boardies", terms which are still used occasionally.

A log book of the Melyn School (this was first established by P. W. Flower the local industrialist and, later, taken over by the School Board; its motto "Manners Makyth Man" was that of Winchester Public School where Flower was educated) provides some depressing details of the conditions prevailing in a school of those times: an entry in February 1900 indicates that there was no fireplace or stove in the classrooms and the children were all congregated in the main room where there was one fire only, during cold weather. Open ventilators, which could not be shut, added to the discomfort.

In Alderman Davies' School, a log book entry, in January 1878, refers to an epidemic raging in the town. Many children were absent and several deaths were reported. Many children were absent and several deaths were reported. Archdeacon Griffiths called at the school and advised all the girls to stay home until the weather improved. There were no fires in the classrooms; no lighting meant that the school was closed before the official time during the winter months. The problem of graffiti was prevalent then as now, as the head-master stated that he usually arrived at school very early to arrange for the removal of obscene remarks made on the walls by those attending evening classes.

In 1899, the Welsh Intermediate Act was passed and a County Intermediate School was built on Cadoxton Road (later to become the Girls' Grammar School) which was opened in 1896 with 74 on roll (mixed). The Balfour Education Act, of 1902, placed all secondary schools under the control of the new County Councils, although a local Board of Governors acted for them exercising far more power than the governing bodies of modern days. A 1905 Report of the Governors showed that, in addition to the general administration, the Governors were also responsible for the financial side. The following figures were quoted:

Grants-in-Aid = £660
Fees from pupils = £940
Sale of books & stationery = £968
The Governors paid all salaries and wages.

In 1907, the Board of Education empowered the County Council to offer free places to enable the less well-off pupils to benefit from secondary education. The percentage of free places was left to the authority and this percentage increased throughout the years with limitations imposed by the size of the schools. In 1928, a new Grammar School for boys was opened at Dwr-y-felin, the girls remaining in the old building.

The 1902 Act placed all elementary education under borough control, acting through an Education Committee. It was eventually designated as a Part III Authority. The abolition of School Boards and the placing of all schools, denominational and otherwise, resulted immediately in fierce controversies in Neath. Non-conformists and similar opinion was very much opposed to the maintenance of Anglican and Roman Catholic Schools out of public rates. Many protest meetings were held and resolutions passed condemning the 1902 Act. One aspect of the conflict was seen in the bitter complaints of the N.U.T. and a teacher councillor (Mr T. Teague), against the disparity of salaries of teachers in state and denominational schools. Teague demanded equal pay for the latter. The Town Council also decided to forward an official protest to the ministry against the act. Yet uniformity of administration was achieved and this had long been the gaol of constitutional reformers.

In 1909, a new school was opened in Brynhyfryd and an Infants' School in Cimla Cwrt Sart School appeared in 1913 (used for a time as a war hospital) Catholic interests had been served much earlier in 1903 with the opening of St Joseph's School in Pendrill Street. In 1909 a school was built in the Cimla for 120 children.

It was however, obvious by 1910 and 1911, that the demand for schools was far exceeding the supply. Since the School Boards were established in 1870, the population had rised from 9,000 to 17,000 by 1911. Overcrowding in schools became a matter of much concern and Councillor J. R. Jones, chairman of the Trades Council, repeatedly raised the matter with the Education Committee. In 1913, an Inspector's report stressed very forcibly the very unsatisfactory conditions in existing schools. Buildings, the responsibility of the County Council, were heavily criticised, but the general administration of schools and the dedicated work of staffs were praised. These were traumatic years for the poorer classes in Neath. Industrial unrest and trade depression caused more suffering. Parish relief figures rose rapidly and school meals for the most needy children were organised. On March 17th, 1912 the managers of the Melyn School decided that not only must a mid-day meal be provided but also a breakfast for those children who had come to school without any. Dr J. Morris, the M.O.H., and school nurses were assiduous in their visits to schools and the doctor continually badgered the authorities concerning the provision of new and better school buildings.

The Hadow Report of 1926 followed up the provisions of the 1918 Education Act and resulted in the provision of a system of secondary education for senior pupils not admitted to the Grammar Schools. Cwrt Sart became a secondary school in 1928 with an allocation of selected pupils. This was followed by a Secondary School in Cadoxton in 1930. Technical Education provision was the next step and, in 1932, the Neath Mining and Technical Institute was opened. The beginnings were modest enough with a staff of two but rapid developments soon took place.

As with so many other functions administered by the Borough, education became integrated into County Council administration after the war. The tripartite system of secondary education, established in 1946, gave way to comprehensive education in 1973. The latest development has been the establishment of Neath Tertiary College in 1982, now termed the Neath College, which embraces a wide range of academic and technical subjects for all ages. There are now some 2,200 full-time and 2,500 part-time students. With this briefest sketches of the vast subject of education, we must now turn to other aspects of municipal activities in the pre-war years.

Housing

There must surely be general agreement, especially amongst participants in local government,that housing provides the main function, and most of the headaches in public administration. The ever increasing demand for houses, the multiplicity of problems connected with the actual building of houses, problems of repairs, reconditioning, slum clearance, house letting, labour problems, finance and the general involvement in planning — these, and increasing centralisation, provide a problem of no mean complexity.

The history of municipal housing began with the passing of the Housing of the Workers Act of 1890,[30] although the Public Health Act of 1872 had resulted in a code of bye-laws controlling building being issued by the Borough Council acting as an Urban Sanitary Authority. The standard of house-building had accordingly risen appreciably in the 1880's. But the rapid increase in population demanded far more houses than private specualtion could provide. The 1890 Act not only gave powers to local authorities to build houses, but, also to apply closing orders and clear the slums which had been created by the unrestricted building which went on up to 1868. However, there was no financial assistance forthcoming from the ministry and nothing was done to implement the Act, although it was agreed to pay the expenses of a council delegation to attend Housing Conferences in London and Paris!

At a meeting of Neath Trades Council and Labour Party in 1902, the chairman Councillor J. R. Jones spoke of the urgent need to implement the 1890 Act. He said that two years ago, a deputation had met the Council on this matter but, as far as he knew, they were still there! Councillor David Davies made a passionate plea that, when houses were built, they should be of an artistic design with adequate garden space back and front and accessibility to parks and open spaces. Garden city planning was appearing at this time (for example at Letchworth) and was beginning to influence thinking on housing development.

In 1901, the first municipally owned houses appeared in Hillside and Coronation Road. This effort was, however, very inadequate and a report in the press, in 1913, described housing conditions as a disgrace to the town. Zoar Row, Penydre and the Green were referred to as particularly black spots. The M.O.H., Dr Morris, reported at this time that the infant mortality rate in the Borough was appalling. It was 13 per 1,000 compared to the average for the country of 11 per 1,000. It was no better, as he claimed than the worst slums of the East End of London. Bad housing conditions were blamed for this but one would have thought the economic depression was also a very significant factor.

A press reporter described his visits to houses as having earthen floors, terribly damp walls, and with little or no sanitation. He described as pathetic the heroic attempts of the housewives to brighten and keep clean such dismal dwellings. In June of the same year, a Professor I. Jones addressed a meeting in the town in which he castigated the council for its neglect of housing regulations.

Eventually, houses were built in Wallace Road in 1915 and Burnside in 1916. By 1919, there were 266 houses built under the 1890 Act. This number included, in addition to the above, houses in Elm Road, Glanymor Street, Brynhyfryd Road and Ruskin Street. The immediate post-war years were difficult for house building. Materials were scarce and so was finance. The vision of 'homes for heroes' was becoming very tarnished indeed. On June 4th, 1920, a public meeting ws convened by the Town Clerk, Mr A. I. Curtiss to consider ways and means of raising money under a Housing Bond Scheme for the 'building of houses for the working class'. Members of the Borough and Rural Councils and representatives of the various businesses and banks of the town were specially invited; one firm declined to send anyone as it had already a plan in operation for helping its employees to build homes. It was stated at the meeting that £30,000 was needed to meet the growing demand but the ministry had made it plain that no financial help would be forthcoming until a Housing Bond Scheme was adopted locally. The attendence was so poor that no decision was reached and the meeting was deferred sine die.

However, in 1922, under Dr Addison and later in 1924, under Mr Wheatley, housing subsidies provided a big impetus to building programmes and, under the 1923 Act, 270 houses were built. These were mainly in the Wellfield area, Groves Road, Cook Rees Avenue, Shelone Terrace, Jenkins Road and additions to the streets already mentioned. The 1924 Act resulted in house building in Addision Road, Greenwood Road, Illtyd Street and Idwal Street. A much bigger wave of building occured under the 1930 Act when 325 houses and flats were erected. Ivy Avenue, Digby Road, Wheatly Road, Giants Grave Road, Jack-y-Du Road, Chamberlain Road, Highfield Road and Regent Street West were inlcuded in this list; there were alsos additions to Brynhyfryd Road and Glanymor Street.

In 1932, a Town Planning Act gave new powers to local authorities for planning but the National Government of the day stopped housing subsidies and decided to concentrate on slum clearance. Private building had, for some years past, recovered the immediate post war slump and a steady development of private residential building continued up to the late thirties.

The immediate post-war years was a period of a desperate housing shortage. The backlog created by the suspension of building during the war, the scarcity of building materials and price inflation led the Government to encourage building as many houses as possible of what materials were available. Hence the prefabricated dwellings at Llantwit and Cwrt Sart. The latter houses were supposed to have been free from corrosion but so many defects developed that they were demolished and new houses were built in Tyla Road and Darren Road. The prefabricated houses at Llantwit were, eventually, demolished and a new housing estate planned.

In 1948, Olive Branch Crescent was built and, in 1953-4, Brynawel, Kingdon Owen Road, Moorland Road and Penbryn houses were being erected followed by Lime Grove flats in 1954. The Roman Way estate was commenced in 1951. In 1958 houses in Beacons View, Bwlch Road and Cwm Nant. Wheately Road, Morgans Road and Victoria Street were added in 1968-9 followed by Gnoll Bank and Fairyland in 1970-72. The experiment of building multi-storey flats was begun in 1956; first the Gorge, then Heol Morfa, the Saltings and Cwm Bedd. The decision to build these blocks had been the subject of much earnest discussion in council and amongst outside bodies. It was a sincere attempt to cope with the urgent needs which led to this building project: but whether so many of this type would have been built if more realistic housing need statistics had been available, is extremely doubtful. What is certain is that many long term social problems relating to this flat-building project remain largely unsolved, despite much urgent consideration given to them over the years.

The standard of houses built after 1968 was determined by a Report of the Parker-Morris Commission. Central heating and adequate storage space were the main factors involved and subsidies on new houses were dependent upon these new standards being adopted. There was also the necessity of conforming to a cost yard-stick laid down by the Ministry. The actual grant was an amount calculated to being the rate of interest on a sum borrowed to build a house, down to an acceptable 4%. It could be argued that there was a serious omission in the Parker-Morris Standard. If roof and wall insulation had been included, it could have meant an enormous saving in heating consumption. Nearly half of Britain's energy consumption goes not to industry but to the heating of buildings, and much of this is wasted because our standards of heating and insulation are among the worst in the world. It has been calculated that as much as 50% of fuel costs could be saved if houses were properly built. And expense? The saving would more than compensate over a period of a few years.

In 1970 plans were formulated for an extensive housing project in the Fairyland area; 81 houses being completed by 1972. The Dyfed Road allotments were removed to a more easterly site to provide for further housing developments.

Housing has extended considerably in recent years both in the private and public sector. The demolition of high rise flats in Giants Grave has taken place and attractive reclamation has been executed. In 1986 the Council's housing stock was 6,090. In 1987 it was 6,045. The decrease is due to the operation of 'Right to Buy', the effort of which has been modified by 'new build'.

Parks

The impressive number of parks and playing fields under corporation ownership today had their genesis back in 1856 when the council acquired what was to be called the Corporation Field. Here football and cricket were played and fairs held up to the time of its conversion into Victoria Gardens Park. This was done to commemorate the Diamond Jubilee of Queen Victoria in 1899.

In 1897, the Castle ruins and grounds were presented to the Borough

Council by Alderman J.H. Rowland. This was then converted into a pleasant little public garden, but which in later years fell into disuse.

The Mount Pleasant gounds were purchsed in 1910 and the corner stone was laid in 1911 by the Mayor David Davies. It was to develop into a very useful amenity to this district and became the home of a very successful Bowls Club. In 1920 the Gnoll Sports Ground was purchased.

During the year 1921, there was much discussion concerning the necessity of a war memorial. Letters, especially from ex-servicemen's organisations, reached the council urging the authority to decide on a memorial and one that would be worthy of the town. Discussions had in fact, been going on regarding this matter and it was finally decided to buy the Gnoll Estate Grounds as a Memorial Park with a memorial gate enscribed on which would be the names of all those who had made the supreme sacrifice in the 1914-18 conflict. The project was to be paid for partly by public subscription and partly by the council. In this way, the town acquired one of the finest natural parks in the country.

The Briton Ferry district is well blessed with the delightful Jersey Park. The land for this was the gift of Lord Jersey made in 1908. The Briton Ferry Estates had come into the possession of this family through a bequest by The Hon. Louisa Mansell, Baroness Vernon (sole heiress of Bussy Lord Mansell, great grandson of Bussy Mansell. the Cromwellian Commander of Glamorgan). The benificiary was W.A.H. Villiers, second son of the Earl of Jersey. His descendent, the 7th Earl, married the daughter of Lord Leigh of Bicester. Amongst other high offices, he was Governor General of New South Wales. The Earl owned 19,000 acres with English seats in Isleworth and Bicester. He and the countess became well known philanthropists. The Earl died in 1915 before the park was opened, which was not until 1925. The opening ceremony was performed by Mrs Alex Clarke, wife of the Borough Engineer. In 1928 a further grant of land for this park and for a Recreation Ground at Brynhyfryd was given by the young Earl of Jersey on attaining his majority in August 1928.

A later addition at amenities at Briton Ferry was the pleasant public walk called Rhodfa Clarke, the result of the council's purchase of the 'incline'. The parks, playing fields and open space amenities have been steadily extended. A new leisure centre is now being planned at the Cwrt Herbert site.

Of the two visible remains of our Medieval past, the Abbey has been for some time a pleasant and interesting place to visit. Excavations in the 1840's were led by the Rector of Neath, the Rev. H. Knight and, in this century, many years of valuable work have been associated with the names of the late Mr G.A. Taylor and late Mr Stanley Thomas (Borough

Archivist). The site was donated to the Ministry of Works in 1949 by the late County Councillor Alan Thomas of Neath Abbey.

The Castle shows every sign of being similarly rehabilitated by the dedicated work of the Neath Antiquarians and with the co-operation of the Borough Council. Our Roman past is echoed by the remains of Nidum with the discovery of which the late Mr Stanley Thomas was intimately connected. It was his discovery of a piece of Samian ware and Roman brick that led to the identification of the Roman Station.

Allotments came into being as a result of food shortage in the first world war, but their appeal was not confined to the production of food. To many, working an allotment provides a healthy and creative hobby, involving no small degree of friendship and sociability.

In the first instance allotments were set up on eleven acres of land leased from the Gnoll estate. It became freehold property in 1923 when the Gnoll Estate was purchsed. An active allotment society took over the administration in consultation with the allotment committee of the council. Other allotments were cultivated in Briton Ferry and adjoining the marsh. Allotments are now in the control of the Community Council.

The men — solidarity forever — of Henllan colliery, Seven Sisters, after the long bitter lock-out of 1926. Beaten into submission, they remained unconquerable in spirit as suggested in this photograph.

Maternity And Child Welfare

One of the most successful voluntary organisations in the Borough of Neath has been the Neath Nursing Association which had been operating in Neath from the early years of the century. Despite a shortage of funds, (constant appeals for subscriptions were made) it carried out an enormous amount of visiting work. In 1910, no fewer than 8,000 visits were made.

In January 1919, the Council decided to set up a Maternity and Child Welfare Committee and to place the service on a public footing, a clinic at first functioned in the Town Hall and then in the Council Chamber. But Dr. Morris was not at all satisfied with the suitability of this building and a new, purpose built clinic was established at Dyfed Road in 1931 which included Health Offices. A clinic in the South Ward was held in St Catherine's Parish Church and in Hunter Street, Briton Ferry. The popularity of these clinics was immense. New special departments were introduced and new medical equipment added to their appeal to the public. Such clinics are held today in most parts of the Borough (The St Catherine's clinic is discontinued).

Library Service

This service expanded considerably in recent years and many discussions took place and resolutions passed in various Library Committee meetings relating to the building of a new library in the town. Eventually, however, a

Neath from the Gnoll: the Mera cottages are on the near edge of Corporation Field (Victoria Gardens from 1899). Left foreground, the last Gnoll Pit, with its smithy to the right, and Greenway 'Cottage', with Forster Road to its right, and the site of the Gnoll Primary School. Background, extreme left, the tram depot with Wesley Chapel (now demolished) to its right.

house adjoining the Central Library was purchased in 1970 and the childrens' library was transferred to this building. This provided much needed space for the extension of the lending library and a complete refurbishment of the whole library took place.

A Record Lending Department established in 1960 had been an instant success and a students' research room supplied a much needed amenity. An important accessory service has been the National Library Lending Scheme whereby books not in stock at Neath can be borrowed through the administrative centre at the National Library, Aberystwyth. If the books needed are not available in the Wales district then application can be made to the National Centre of Boston Spa in Yorkshire.

The total issue of books of all kinds in Neath and Briton Ferry in the year 1973-4 was 264,000 compared with 13,000 in 1924.

For 1986 there were 31,043 books in stock and 238,700 books issued.

There is also an extensive Reference Library which includes a local history and manuscript section.

The Police

The Police System in non-county boroughs like Neath continued to be controlled by the Watch Committee up to the immediate post-war years. The committee was responsible for all aspects of Police administration. Unlike the county, they could appoint a chief constable without the approval of the Home Office.

After the Local Government Acts of the latter years of the Nineteenth Century the Police System developed steadily. The Police Station was moved from the cramped unhygienic quarters in James Street to the old Town Hall, where new cells were installed. One of the arguments used by the Police for these cells was that it was embarrassing to wheel 'drunks' in handcarts to the cells in James Street in full public view especially if those conveyed were females!

In 1902, a pension scheme was established and conditions and pay gradually improved. Hours of work, however, continued to be very long being from 6 a.m. to 9 p.m. and at night, from 9 p.m. to 6 a.m.

For ceremonial purposes horses were hired and mounted police always made a big impression in the town. In 1908 a report by Chief Constable Higgins revealed an establishment of 18 officers, including 4 sergeants, 13 constables and the chief constable which was one officer to 916 of the population (slightly below authorised strength). The usual Certificate of Efficiency from the Home Office was included.

It was not until the findings of the Desborough Committee, in 1919, were implemented, that the Police Force was placed on anything like a

Neath Police, c. 1902. Reproduced from an old photograph. *(By permission of the Neath Antiquarian Society).*

modern footing with a uniform system of pay and general conditions. One recommendation was that the police should be transferred to the County Authority as the impersonal character of a large authority would be more conducive to discipline and flexibility of staff and, therefore, for promotion prospects.

This is exactly what happened in the immediate post-war years, bringing to an end an excellent record of dedicated service to the community on the part of the Borough Police.

The Committee System

Ever since the beginning of modern local government in 1835, the committee has been the pivot of its operation. Only one, the Watch Committee, was formed under the Reform Act (the name was derived from the 'Watch and Ward' duty of earlier centuries) which was to administer the Police Service. By 1914, the large increase in functions inevitably meant a proliferation of committees. By 1914, the Library, Market and Slaughterhouse, Housing, Education Halls, Music, Electricity, Streets, Cattle Disease and Watch Committees were functioning. To these Allotments and Child & Maternity Welfare were to be added after the war. Powers of co-option were enjoyed by the Library, Education and Welfare Committees.

A right relationship between committee and officers is a matter of fundamental importance to the proper functioning of local government and this has always existed in Neath with very few exceptions. The increasing complexity of modern administration had become more and more challenging to council members and the role of the officer is perhaps destined to be more prominent. Yet it will alway be true (in the words of Laski) that 'the largest objects of public policy are a matter in which the amateur's conception of what constitutes the welfare of the community remains supreme'.

Rating

The term "rates" is, surely, one of the most emotive words in the public mind. No payment is made with greater reluctance. There are many reasons for this but perhaps one of the chief ones is the difficulty of the ratepayer to relate the payment of rates to what is provided. Another basis of criticism from some sections is that rating is based on property valuations: but of all the alternative schemes suggested, including one involving a local income tax, none has found general acceptance up to now.

Rating is, of course, a vital part of local administration and none of the developing utilities and amenities does not involve money, either in annual expenses or capital charges.

The most important milestone in rating reform since the Goschen proposals of 1888, was the 1929 Local Government Act of Mr Neville Chamberlain. He was a much criticised Prime Minister but, as Minister of Health, he was the architect of notable reforms in the sphere of local government. After dealing with the abolition of the Guardians and the transfer of their functions to the County Councils, he turned his attention to finance. Mr Winston Churchill, Chancellor of the Exchequer, had worked into the Bill certain provisions, such as the relief of rates to industry. So the Act was partly a compromise yet it introduced major reforms. There was now to be an annual exchequer grant to every authority which was to be fixed for five years. It was based on needs rather than the size of the community. The new grant would have reference to low rateable value, unemployment and the density of population. Industrial concerns were relieved of 75% of their rates and agricultural land and outbuildings were totally exempt. A consolidated rate and a simplication of grants brought order into the rating system. Mr Arthur Greenwood, the new Minister of Health in 1929, appointed a committee to codify many of the local government Acts and in 1933, 1936 and 1938 further legislation simplified local administration. A new power was given to councils to delegate executive power to certain committees if they wished, a power which was not implemented in Neath.

The Period 1940-1972

There were no elections during the war years and vacancies were filled by co-option.

Council work was confined to basic functions and central control became, inevitably, very dominant especially in matters such as Civil Defence. New powers and functions were almost all of a temporary nature, yet, during this time, an immense amount of planning for reconstruction in many fields took place and the immediate post war years was a period of almost an unequalled amount of national legislation in a wide range of spheres. It is one of the ironies of history that wars, which result in almost unimaginable human misery, almost invariably produce a climate making for fundamental reforms.

The only Act however, passed during the War was R. A. Butlers' Education Act of 1944. This transferred the whole of public education (except that in the County Boroughs) to the county authorities although the creation of Divisional Executive authorities enabled local regions to play their part in the reconstruction schemes. The chief purpose of the Act was to provide secondary education for all according to age, aptitude and ability. Parity of esteem was aimed at between the three types of secondary schools established, Grammar, Technical and Secondary Modern. The school leaving age was raised to 15 and provision made for a future rise to 16. In the Borough, two secondary modern schools were established in 1953, at Pencaerau and the Gnoll. All age schools now disappeared with the exeption of St Josephs. Not many years were to ensue before ideas of comprehensive education began to ferment in the public mind. There was, of course, a whole philosophy, involving not only educational but also social ideals, in the concept of the Comprehensive School; but the predominant motive was a growing consciousness of the iniquities of the 11+ examination which was tending to produce more neurosis in parents than in the children. The transference of the senior pupils of St Josephs' to the new Comprehensive School in Port Talbot and of Welsh pupils to the Welsh Comprehensive School in Ystalyfera (preceded by Glynneath pupils attending Rhyfelin in Pontypridd) gave this district its first taste of comprehensive education.

The flight from local government was seen in many spheres apart from education. Gas and electricity passed from municipal control to National Boards organised on a regional basis. Health and the Police also departed from Borough administration. But, whilst in terms of actual numbers of functions, the responsibility of the Borough Council was less, the increasing complexity of modern legislation relating to the powers that remained meant there was more than less pressure on time spent by members carrying out their duties.

This complexity of modern municipal government is seen particularly in the sphere of finance and it has not been lessened by the lack of any systematic and consistent ideas which might have led to more coherence on the subject.

The story of grants, for instance, since 1945 has been one of "patching and mending" whilst proposals for a radical reform have been consistently deferred. Several systems of finance have been tried out since the war; a matter of one temporary expedient succeeding the other.

One factor which stands out is that local authorities have been receiving an increasing percentage of their total income from grants compared with that received from rates. In 1945, rates were approximately equal to grants. In 1968, the amount of grants received from the Ministry was 7% higher than the sum produced by rates. A new valuation of property was made in 1963 based on current values. Places where there was little or no industry were badly hit. Then in 1968 two reforms were introduced to lessen the burden on the householder; one was to allow a rate rebate to the very low income groups; the other was to introduce a lower rate in the pound for domestic and other property compared with industry.

In respect of government grants an attempt was made in 1948 to lift the poorer areas up to the average wealth of local authorities (wealth being equated with the rateable value per head of the population). This was done by replacing the general Exchequer Grant (or the Block Grant) by an Equalisation Grant. Thinly populated areas received a small addition and children over 15 were counted twice. The result was that some authorities received 25% of their local budget and others as much as 75%.

In 1957, a new system of grants was introduced. Industry would have to pay 50% of its rates instead of 25%. But the most important factor was that grants for specific purposes were abolished and a general grant was to operate. Authorities would now be free to spend where they saw fit. Educationists were alarmed because they feared that education would suffer in competing for money with other demands.

Eventually resources became more limited and Mr Crossman introduced a Bill which meant that an estimate of total local expenditure for two years would have to be submitted and a total grant would be fixed as a proportion of that sum. Industry would pay its full complement although agriculture would still enjoy exemption from rates on land and outbuildings.

In terms of a rate-support grant, Neath received an average percentage grant of 25.5%. Details of the 1966-72 years are as follows.

Year	Grant	% Grant
1971-72	£146,535	25.02
1970-71	£153,609	24.88
1969-70	£137,225	26.31
1968-69	£110,997	25.16
1967-68	£111,373	26.25
1966-67	£ 92,944	25.19
Averages	£125,447	25.5

Central Government pay grants to local authorities to help them pay for services. In this year the Neath Borough Council received 2.9 million pounds in rate support grant. This is 66% of its total expenditure.

Summary of the Government Grant Allocation 1981/1987

Prior to 1981 the rate support grant consisted of a needs element and a resources element. In 1981 the government introduced a new system which merged the two separate elements into one block grant. This new system was designed to make expenditure targets specific to individual authorities, with grant penalties affecting individual authorities if they spent more than their target. In 1986/1987 the system was further changed. The targets were shelved and replaced by a system whereby an authority would lose a greater amount of grant the more it spent. The amount of grant received by Neath Borough Council over this period is illustrated below:

Details of the years 1981-1987 are as follows:

	Grant Received £000	Grant as a Percentage of Net Revenue Expenditure
1981-1982	2477	64.24%
1982-1983	2626	70.57%
1983-1984	3016	82.79%
1984-1985	2461	67.28%
1985-1986	2522	67.8 %
1986-1987	2392	50.85%

Town Planning

What sort of town did we want to see developing and how best could the resources available be used? Those were among the many questions posed in the formative years after the war.

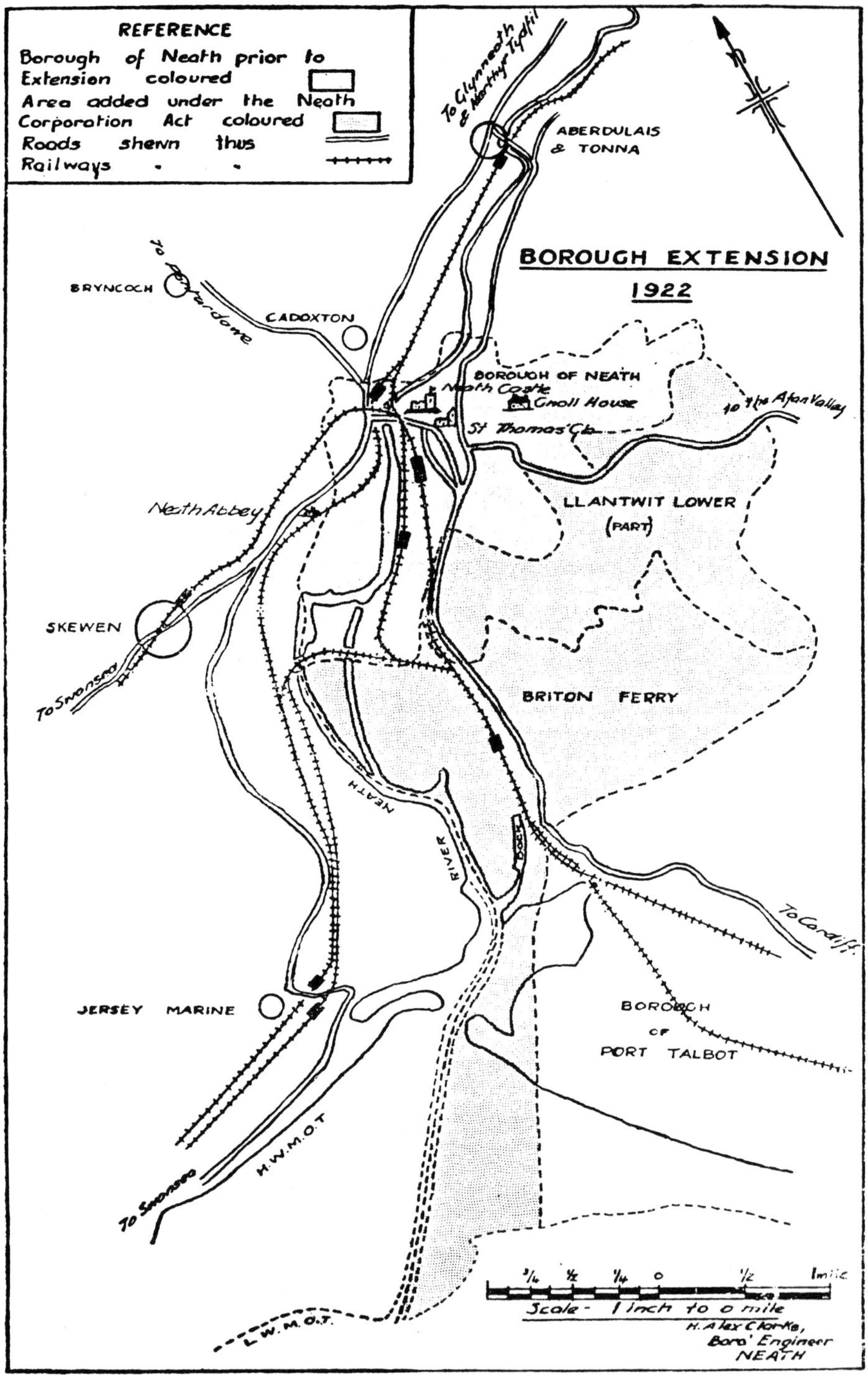

Borough extension 1922.

The County Council was given the responsibility for planning (under the 1948 Act) and it became their duty to prepare a development plan for each area, defining how land might best be used. In 1958, a plan for Neath was completed embracing the Borough and part of the adjoining land under the Rural District Council. This was called the "Town Map". The whole area was designated for residential, business, shopping, industrial, office and warehouse purposes. Elsewhere, plans had already been executed but they were in towns which had been extensively damaged from air-raids (Swansea, for example) and, for these, substantial grants had been allotted. Later, in 1966, a more detailed map relating to town centre redevelopment in Neath was prepared. This became known as the "2001 Map" and it involved, amongst other factors, the planning of a pedestrian precinct and circulatory traffic system. The piece-meal extension of the Heads-of-the-Valley Road had meant the planning of a trunk road from Aberdulais to Llandarcy. Various alignments were considered for this but the final one adopted was one which cut through Bridge Street thus closing the centuries old traditional entry into Neath from the North. Involved in this scheme, was a Southern Link Road connecting up with the new trunk road by means of an interchange on the marsh and providing an entry into the town from the North and West at Stockham's Corner. Here a major roundabout would provide a fulcrum incorporating the circulatory traffic flow round the town.

The scheme was opposed, at a Public Inquiry held in March 1970, by the Borough, and other bodies and individuals. The basis of the Borough's protest (the result of a majority decision on the Council) was that a Northern Link was preferable as it would avoid the distinction of over a hundred homes and the run-down of the Northern part of the town. The plan of the Welsh Office and County Council (which had been opposed by local members of the county authority) was upheld by the Ministry Inspector but he recommended that a Northern Link be built simultaneously with the Southern Link to avoid the partial cul-de-sac created in the North part of the town by the closing of Bridge Street.

The involvement in planning by the Borough Council was the result of planning powers delegated to it by the County Council thus reversing, in a small measure, the "fight from local government" which has already been noted. The first delegated agreement was drawn up in 1948 followed by a final agreement in 1964. Powers were given to the Borough to "excercise and perform planning functions on behalf of the County Council". However, plans dealt with by the Borough had to be "in accord" with the general development plans laid down by the County. The latter also reserved the right to instruct the Borough Council to consult with them when it was desired. In other words, the county remained very much in control.

The driving force behind the new road plans was not simply the increase in traffic but the rate of increase. In 1953, the Briton Ferry Bridge was opened to relieve through town traffic. It was strongly opposed in the town as it was thought that Neath would be by-passed by shoppers. But the weekly increase in cars not only made no difference to town traffic but soon began to cause problems of congestion despite the bridge. Be that as it may, too often in the minds of planners the motor-car is "king" and human considerations secondary or completely disregarded. There is some point in the famous cartoon in which a Ministry Official is depicted informing a householder that a road would be brought to his door, but that first of all, his home would have to be demolished.

Main Drainage

Periodic flooding had, over the years, caused great havoc and distress to many householders in Neath and it was decided to embark on a gigantic scheme to replace an antiquated drainage and sewerage system. Up to March 1972, the sum of £1,200,000 had been expended on the scheme but, before it is completed, a further £3,000,000 will have to be spent. At present, untreated sewage is still being pumped into the sewer from Aberdulais to the Briton Ferry Wharf, and flooding is still not completely conquered. The whole plan cannot be completed too quickly.

In 1960, water administration passed to the Water Board and later, in 1971-2, plans were formulated for a new Water Authority to be set up which would also take over drainage and the River Board's responsibilities, with the Borough Council acting as agent.

The Neath Borough Council acts as agent for the Water Authority. At present the long sea outfall provide for the former Borough whilst the Rural area is serviced by treatment plants and river outfalls.

Fairs

The oldest institution in Neath is the Fair. It is as old, almost, as the Borough itself and it is still with us. Very few towns in Wales, or indeed in Britain, has this institution so deeply entrenched into its way of life.

From three fairs granted by the Charters the number increased to at least nine in the last century; wool and flannel fairs in March and October, horse and cattle fairs in May, Trinity Wednesday, July and November and the Great September Fair established since 1880 to be held on the second Thursday of the month. There were, also, Hiring Fairs attached to many of these. To modern eyes, they savoured in many ways of the slave market

where would-be servants lined up to be chosen by farmers and others for service at usually £10 a year and keep for seven days a week. A fair in Briton Ferry (sited near the Railway Station) flourished in the latter part of the nineteenth century.

The Neath Fair was held on the Corporation Field from 1856 to 1896 when Victoria Gardens Park was established. It then was transferred to the Bird-in-Hand Field leased from Mr Evans-Bevan. In the 1960's, the site was earmarked for the new Civic Centre and the Fair found its present home not far from the castle walls, against which the first fair snuggled in the dangerous years of the far-off thirteenth century. There were periods when public interest in the Fair waned. Such a time was around the year 1900, but the coming of such novelties as cinematograph shows restored much of the attaction.

Gradually, the pleasure side of the fair began to predominate and street stalls by outside traders replaced the old commercial fair. The days of the colourful drovers and of the Hiring Fair vanished with the coming of the twentieth century. Eventually, even the picturesque and much welcomed

A cricket match between the United South of England and a Neath/Cadoxton cricket team in 1868 at the Gnoll. In this match the famous W. G. Grace was bowled in both innings without scoring. The bowler was Howitt, a professional cricketer from England and on this occasion a guest bowler for the Neath/Cadoxton team. For this game the Welsh team had 22 players against the English team's 11 players.

"Merched y Mera" with their baskets of cockles disappeared from the scene. The weekly mart now caters for farmers but the Fair itself is still very much part of the autumn scene in Neath and much of the old magic still lingers on. Today we find the Pleasure Fair in a new site (British Rail sidings) but its attraction survives. For further details see 'The Story of Neath Fair' (by the present writer).

The Civic Centre

The first Civic Centre in Neath was the Castle where the administration of the Borough was carried on in a timbered hall within the castle court-yard. Almost nine centuries later another Civic Centre was to be built not many hundreds of yards away reflecting, by its very nature, some of the changes which the intervening centuries had brought about.

It was during the year 1935 that ideas of a new administrative building were first seriously discussed but the spectre of costs was upper-most and it was not until the early sixties that plans for a new Civic Centre in the Bird-in-Hand Field were made. This was to be a purpose-built cente to replace the many adminstrative buildings disseminated about the town used by the Borough and the Rural District Councils.

The winning architectural design was the work of Mr Kenneth Hathaway of Kent which carried with it a prize of £3,000. The site was donated by Sir David Evans-Bevan who also made a cash gift of £10,000 and furnished the Mayor'r Room. The Members' Room was furnished by the Metal Box Company and a fountain was provided by the British Aluminium Company. This comprised a metal aluminium crystal magnified 25,000 times.

In view of reorganisation, it was a happy foresight that the building was planned to house the two authorities and, today, it adds dignity to a town which is not too well blessed with attractive buildings. A new centralised reception area has been added which contributes much to the efficiency of the Civic administration.

The Civic Centre and its Works of Art

The new Civic Centre has acquired an imposing array of art treasures reflecting a great variety of artistic work, some of which reflects a high standard.

The majority of works reflects the extraordinary period in the history of art between the middle of the eighteenth century and the middle of the nineteenth century. It was a period when waves of drawings of landscapes and scenes of topographical interest. The landed gentry were anxious to have their homes and estates depicted by artists as this was the age before

Aquaduct over the River Neath by I. G. Wood, 1811. *(By permission of the NLW).*

the camera. Furthermore the decline of religion at that time led artists and poets to turn to the divinity in nature as a subject for their art.

A description of the artists involved include William Delamotte (1780-1863), P. Sandley (1725-1809), Thomas Hornor (1785-1844), Buck Bros, C. W. Hampion, W. Baxter, I. G. Wood, S. Middiman, J. Humfray, Henrock Cort, J. B. Smith (Waterfall Smith) and Benjamin West and their paintings can be found in the publication "The Civic Centre and its Works of Art" published by the Borough Council and written by the author of these pages. Besides the paintings referred to, the collection includes modern paintings by artists. One of national reputation such as Neath's Will Roberts.

The Council and Cultural Activities

There are few towns (if, indeed any) of the size of Neath with such a splendid range of cultural societies especially in the field of music. The Borough Council has, for many years made financial grants to many of these organisations and, through its Music Committee, sponsored many concerts particularly by our youth orchestras and choirs. The range of its support is extending, this being indicative of its ever-developing civic consciousness. An Arts Centre must surely be a future development.

Dyfed Road Baths

The opening of the Swimming Pool in September 1961 conferred on the Town and all the outlying districts an amenity of immense value to people of all ages.

Every year its popularity has increased. Apart from general recreational use by the public, schools have made much use of the Baths through organised visits. Approximately, 1500 children receive swimming instruction each year and 75% were able to swim after 4 to 5 weeks tuition. Over 500 adults every year receive lessons and the majority are able to swim after the first 8 lessons. Handicapped children are also helped. The Baths Superintendent and his excellent staff hope to develop this activity. A popular accessory to the establishment is the Sauna Bath facility and increasing use is being made of this.

Life-saving has played a prominent part in the Bath's activities and many Bronze, Elementary and Water Safety awards by the Royal Life Saving Society have been won.

The Press

Visitors to Tenby, that most beautiful resort in Britain, will perhaps have noticed a plaque outside the offices of the "Weekly Observer" which has the following inscription.

> "A Press Freedom Pioneer — A former owner and Editor of this newspaper Mr Frank. B. Mason, found the doors of the Borough Council Chamber locked against him in March, 1907, because of his critical comments of the Council.
>
> He obtained a court injunction against the Council but the judgement was reversed by the High Court. Three Judges of Appeal laid down that the Press had no legal right of admission to report meetings of public authorities or of Parliament.
>
> As a direct result of the national publicity given to Frank. B. Mason's litigation, the Admission of the Press Act of 1908 was passed."

This event must surely take a proud place in Tenby's rich history (like Neath it was one of the ancient boroughs established by the Normans) for the freedom of the Press is part of democracy itself and it has always been one of the first victims of the dictator. That, in itself, is one of the finest tributes that can be paid it.

Protests against the exclusion of the Press from Neath Council Meetings in the last century were made in no uncertain terms by journalists who also expressed what they thought the authority should be doing for the good government of the town. On March 26th, 1858, a "Cambrian" reporter described what he considered the poor state of the town as "compatible with excluding the Press and conducting its business in secret . . . the do-nothing system is triumphant with the councillors and notions of making people happier than they are, are absent, so why are they there? The reason is that no one knows what goes on. Plenty of canvassing, a good supply of beer and no reported meetings. Halcyon Days!"

The Neath Council followed the fairly general practice of allowing the Press to attend Monthly Council Meetings where information was extracted from the Council Meetings regarding the various committees which were held during the month. After the last war, many of the changes which occurred in the sphere of local government included the admission of reporters to all main committees except those of Finance, Parliamentary and Staff; a restriction which was to be removed under the 1972 Act. As far as the public were concerned, a public gallery was provided in the new Civic Centre. There is a well known legal dictum that where the Press goes the public can go and there is, certainly, logic in this.

Relations between Press and Council in Neath have always been generally on a high note and journalists have always co-operated with members when it has been necessary to "go into Committee" or to refrain from (for instance Neath Borough Reorganisation, Recreational Act, A Million Pound Scheme, Urban Development) reporting an item which might hamper negotiations.

The Neath Borough since Reorganisation

In the period since 1973, the spectre of unemployment has gradually overshadowed the Borough. Rheola Works has now disappeared and a severe reduction in the work force in the Metal Box Factory has taken place. A severe blow has been dealt also by the almost complete closure of the Llandarcy Oil Refinery. Today unemployment stands at 15%.

Efforts to mitigate this tragedy have been strenuous. Small workshops have been set up in Lonlas, Glynneath and the Neath Abbey Business Park. These have been planned and financed by the Borough Council and administered by the Neath Development Partnership. This organisation was initiated by Thomson International Ltd and was formed by repres-

The Middle Clun Gwyn waterfalls near Pont-Nedd-Fechan, Vale of Neath, West Glam. *(By permission of the Neath Development Partnership Enterprise Ltd.).*

entatives of the Borough Council, Trade Unions and nominated associates. The Partnership was eventually incorporated into a limited company called the Neath development Partnership Enterprise Ltd. Since its inception in 1983 it has now been basically restructured, many changes having been made mainly in personnel.

Other organisations have been involved in youth training for future possible employment. One is the Neath Borough Training Agency with its two year course for young people (16-19) aimed at training in a variety of skills. We have also the Information Technology Centre where workshop training takes place in basic word processing techniques, soft ware and hard ware assembly, servicing and repairs. From I.T.E.C. and the Training Agency, some proceed to the Neath College.

Tourism has been part of the Partnership activities and few towns have such a wealth of natural attractions as Neath. Wooded valleys with magnificent waterfalls, forest walks, canal paths (restored by the Canal preservation Society) splendid attractions such as the Penscynor Wild Life Park, Cefn Coed Steam and Coal Museum and the Seven Sisters Museum. Developments in tourist attractions have been such as the Neath Council was awarded the second prize in the recent National Trust Award.

Recreational Activities

A comprehensive account of these appear in the official Borough Guide. Since its publication however, new developments are planned in the Gnoll Grounds mainly with the help of the Manpower Service Commission. The restoration of the Cascade north of the Moss-House reservoir has been completed (this was constructed in the 1970's and in the informal style of landscaping that replaced the French style). The recent plans include internal road improvements, car parks, a cafeteria and dredging ponds. A preliminary meeting with the Countryside Commission revealed the possibility that the Gnoll Estate might acquire the status of a Country Park and thus qualifying for a 50% grant.

A Million Pound Scheme

A new and exciting contribution to the unemployment problem has been the setting up of a million pound plan at B.P.'s Llandarcy. The Llandarcy Development Ltd (after William Know D'arcy the founder of the Refinery in 1923) would operate the scheme, co-ordinating all existing job creation efforts and working closely with the Borough Council, West Glamorgan, the W.D.A. and the Welsh T.U.C. The vital fact about this plan is that it will provide more jobs than were lost in the recent restucturing.

Renovation of canal and lock at Resolven by the Neath Development Partnership and Agency (with help from the Borough Council). Work is planned at three other locations (Creigiau, Rheola and Aberclwyd). *(By permission of Philip Doré).*

Urban Development

An ambitious urban development plan is emerging involving the private and public sector embracing housing, shopping, businesses and recreation. Central to this is the construction of a northern link. This 17 million pound scheme will mean major reconstruction of the northern part of the town.

A new traffic alignment would take place and the road through the Millands connecting with the urban by-pass is planned. Transport developments include motorways between Baglan and Lonlas and between Aberdulais and Glynneath.

The complex story of the evolution of Neath as a borough has now reached its conclusion. The genesis of our town with its Castle-Church nucleus was a characteristic achievement of the Normans in their policy of colonisation of the land they conquered. These Frenchmen of Viking blood became a symbol of power and authority but, before the end of the Middle Ages, they became like so many other conquerors, absorbed in the race that they had conquered. They vanished as a people although a lingering prestige survives in the boast by some people of their alleged Norman blood.

The Borough established by them survived and evolved; slowly and painfully in the Middle Ages, quicker and more confidently under the Tudors and Stuarts; finally, despite a complete domination by the Mackworths in the 18th century, achieving its first bloom of maturity in the 19th century as a democratically elected Municipal Corporation expressing its civic consciousness in a multiplicity of functions for the common good.

The Borough in its early years could be described as the urban part of the member-lordship of Neath. The amalgamation with the Rural Council formed new boundaries which were largely those of the ancient Lordship thus turning the wheel full circle. The coming of the northern link and the inner urban renewal will mean the re-birth of the old submerged area of the town and a secondary historical cycle will have taken place.

Demographically, Neath is an amalgum of immigrants from mainly neighbouring counties, especially Dyfed and from Cornwall, Devon and Somerset, integrating with the indigenous Welsh.

If we were asked what was the real purpose of our developing Borough, the answer to three questions would be the basis of such an asessment. Is it efficient? Is it economical? Above all, does it add to the quality of life for everyone?

Appendix

Appendix A

A List of Provosts and Portreeves (C1100-1835)

Compiled from "The History of Neath Abbey", (W. Birch), "The History of the Vale of Neath", (D. R. Phillips), the Municipal Centenary Handbook 1835-1935 (notes by G. A. Taylor) and corporation records.

1200	Alfred.
1296	Peter de Straddelaye.
1298	Walter Kacheurens.
1300	William Peres.
1329	Elias Trons.
1331	John Crugan.
1332	David Appedoun.
1521	Ieuan Lloyd.
1648	David Price.
1665	David Leyshon.
1666	David Price.
1667-9	David Leyshon.
1680	Thomas Hopkin.
1681	Howel Leyshon.
1682	Thomas Hopkin.
1683	Thomas Hopkin.
1684	Thomas Hopkin.
1685	John Llewellyn.
1688	Thomas Basset.
1692	Henry Howell.
1693	Thomas Hopkin.
1697	Thomas Cralph.
1699	Jacob Davies.
1702	Benjamin Price.
1706	John Davies.
1707	John Davies.
1708	Leyson Hopkin
1709	Richard Thomas.
1713	Leyson Hopkin.
1717	Leyson Hopkin.
1719	Richard Thomas.
1720	Richard Thomas.
1725	John Llewellyn.
1726	Richard Thomas.
1727	Richard Thomas.
1731	John Hopkin.
1732	John Hopkin.
1733	John Llewllyn.
1734	Richard Thomas.
1736	Richard Thomas.
1737	William Gabb.
1738	William Gabb.
1740	William Gabb.
1743	David Watkins.
1747	R. Weaver.
1748	R. Weaver.
1749	William Gabb.
1750	Joseph Bosworth.
1753	William Howell.
1758	William Howell.
1759	William Howell.
1760	William Howell.

1761	William Spicket.
1762	William Spicket.
1763	Herbert Mackworth.
1764	William Cross.
1765	William Cross.
1766	David Hopkins.
1767	David Hopkins.
1768	Henry Griffiths.
1769	Henry Griffiths.
1770	Thomas Hopkins.
1771	Thomas Hopkins.
1772	Llewellyn Price.
1773	Richard Weaver.
1774	William Cross.
1775	William Cross.
1776	William Cross.
1777	Thomas David.
1778	Thomas David.
1779	Thomas Lewis.
1780	Thomas Lewis.
1781	Thomas Hopkins.
1782	Thomas Hopkins.
1783	William Cross.
1784	William Cross.
1785	Thomas David.
1786	Thomas Hopkin.
1787	Thomas Hopkin.
1788	Thomas Hopkin.
1789	Evan Powell.
1790	Evan Powell.
1791	Evan Robson.
1792	John Mills.
1793	Edward Robson.
1795	Thomas Edwards.
1796	Daniel Benbow.
1797	Richard Pendrill.
1798	Richard Pendrill.
1799	Thomas Edwards.
1800	Rees Rees.
1801	Thomas Leyson.
1802	William Gronow.
1803	Alexander Cuthertson.
1803	Thomas Edwards.
1804	Richard Pendrill.
1805	John King.
1806	Benjamin Howell.
1807	John Morgan.
1808	William Gronow.
1809	Daniel Benbow.
1810	James Coke.
1811	Rees Rees.
1812	Thomas Edwards.
1813	Benjamin Howell.
1814	Henry John Grant.
1815	Thomas Edwards.
1816	Benjamin Howell.
1817	John Morgan.
1818	James Coke.
1819	James Coke.
1820	James Coke.
1821	David Morgan.
1822	David Morgan.
1823	David Morgan.
1824	Henry John Grant.
1825	Benjamin Howell.
1826	David Powell.
1827	George Dods.
1828	Henry John Grant.
1829	Henry John Grant.
1830	Charles Warde.
1831	Benjamin Howell.
1832	David Morgan.
1833	David Morgan.
1834	David Powell.
1835	David Powell.

B List of Mayors 1835-1972

1836	Henry John Grant.
	Thomas Dumayne Place.
1837	John Rowland.
1838	Charles Warde.
1839	John Rowland (vice).
	Charles Warde (resigned).

1839	John Rowland.
1840	Robert Place Leyson.
1841	Thomas Dumayne Place.
1842	Howel Gwyn.
1843	Robert Place Leyshon.
1844	Howel Gwyn.
1845	D. H. Morgan.
1846	Sankey Garder.
1847	Henry Thomas.
1848	Robert Place Leyshon.
1849	Sankey Gardner (vice). Robert Place Leyshon (dec'd Aug).
1849	Sankey Gardner.
1850	Alexander Cuthbertson.
1862	Evan Evans.
1863	William Morgan.
1864	Pendrill Charles.
1865	John Henry Rowland.
1866	Sankey Gardner.
1867	William John Player.
1868	Thomas Andrew.
1869	Howel Chuthbertson.
1870	Henry Lake.
1871	John Henry Rowland.
1872	David Bevan.
1873	David Bevan.
1874	James Kempthorne.
1875	James Kempthorne.
1876	Rowland Thomas.
1877	Richard Bartlett.
1878	Pendrill Charles.
1879	John Henry Rowland.
1880	John Henry Rowland.
1881	David Davies.
1882	Rowland Thomas.
1883	Rowland Thomas.
1884	David Davies.
1885	Thomas Phillips.
1886	John Henry Rowland.
1887	John Rees.
1888	John Bevan Davies.
1889	John Arnold.
1890	William Burrows.
1891	James Davies Llewellyn.
1892	Evan Evans-Bevan.
1894	Hopkin Morgan.
1895	Hopkin Jones.
1896	Arthur Russell Thomas.
1897	Abraham George.
1898	James Glass.
1899	Pendrill Charles.
1900	Lewis Cobden Thomas.
1901	Pendrill Charles.
1902	Evan Evans-Bevan.
1903	Evan Evans-Bevan.
1904	Evan Evans-Bevan.
1905	Walter E. Rees.
1906	Ed. Sincock Phillips.
1907	John Walter Thomas.
1908	Sir Griffiths Thomas Kt.
1909	David Davies.
1910	David Llewellyn Davies.
1911	Hopkin Morgan.
1912	Daniel Harry.
1913	William Burrows Trick.
1914	Matthew Arnold.
1915	Thomas Jones.
1916	Pendrill Charles.
1917	Hopkin Morgan.
1918	John Rees.
1919	John Rowland Jones.
1920	John Davies.
1921	Hopkin Morgan.
1922	Mathias Groves Roberts.
1923	Joseph Cook Rees.
1924	Richard Jenkins.
1925	David Chas. Davies.
1926	William John Hill.
1927	William Kindon Owen.
1928	John Davies.
1929	George Gethin.
1930	William John Challacombe.
1931	Benjamin R. Bowen.

1932	Joseph Branch.
1933	Ernest J. Hopes.
1934	Thomas Cole.
1935-36	George Davies.
1936-37	Jno. Benjamin Williams.
1937-38	Cecil R. Hedge.
1938-39	Edward Chas. Hutchinson.
1939-40	David Chas. Griffiths.
1940-41	William Jnu. Morgan.
1941-42	John Shea.
1942.43	John Emlyn Emmanuel.
1943-44	James Hitchings.
1944-45	Thomas Hughes.
1945-46	Fredk. W. Loader.
1946-47	Philip Howells.
1947-49	Eleazor Thomas. (Extension due to Mayoral appointment being changed from November to May).
1940-50	S. Leonard Burton.
1950-51	Rowland Perrott.
1951-52	Benjamin Morris.
1952-53	W. Reginald Francis.
1953-54	John Walter Jones.
1954-55	William T. Phillips.
1955-56	Gilbert Rosser.
1956-57	Richard Smith.
1957-58	Percy A. Bishop.
1958-59	Francis S. Evans.
1959-60	G. Howard Davies.
1960-61	William S. Watkins.
1962-63	T. Ernest Molland.
1963-64	Jas. Aneurin Rees.
1964-65	Hilda G. Howells.
1965-66	Idris G. Tallamy.
1966-67	Mary Ann Moule.
1967-68	Meuric L. Thomas.
1968-69	R. Lloyd Davies.
1969-70	Leslie Morris.
1970-71	Walter R. Hopes.
1971-72	Gerald Hemmings.
1972-73	W. Roy Hopes.
1973-74	George H. Eaton.
1974-75	J. E. Emmanuel.
1975-76	M. R. Jeffreys.
1976-77	L. C. Adams.
1977-78	M. Thomas J.P.
1979-80	A. D. Powell.
1980-81	W. J. Brown.
1981-82	W. H. Cotton.
1983-84	R. G. Day.
1984-85	R. Bennett J.P.
1985-86	C. James.
1986-87	Mrs I. Hobbs.
1987-88	H. Thomas.

Recipients of the Freedom of the Borough.

Henry Pendrill Charles. 1900
Sir Samuel Thomas Evans K.C.M.P. (Solicitor General). 1908.
The Rt. Hon. David Lloyd George (Prime Minister). 1918.
Evan Evans-Bevan. 1923.
Hopkin Morgan. 1923.
Ernest James Rollings. 1932.
The Rt. Hon. Hugh Dalton (Chancellor of the Exchequer). 1946.
David Martyn Evans Bevan. 1949.
Alfred Edwin Ivor Curtiss. 1954.
Neath Rugby Football club. 1971.

Appendix B

List of Freemen of the Borough

Henry Pendrill Charles 1900
Sir S. T. Evans, K.C.M.P. Solicitor General
The Rt Hon. David Lloyd George (Prime Minister) 1918
Evan Evans-Bevan 1923
Hopkin Morgan 1923
Ernest James Rollings 1932
Hugh Dalton (Chancellor of the Exchequer 1948)
David Martyn Evans-Bevan 1949
Alfred Edwin Curtis 1954
Neath Rugby Football Club 1971
John Emlyn Emannuel 1979
Walter Redvers Hope 1984
Ivor K. Thorne 1886

Appendix C

Administration

Neath Borough Council
Chief Executive — G. H. Griffiths
Borough Secretary — R. H. Rees
Borough Treasurer — S. Penny
Borough Engineer and Planning Officer — A. Jenkins
Chief Environmental Officer — J. H. James
Borough Housing Officer — Mrs E. Bladon
Parks Superintendent — D. Smith
The Borough consists of 34 members
There are 14 Community Councils
Members of Parliament
Neath Constituency — Donald Coleman, C.B.E., J.P., M.P.
European Member of Parliament — David Morris

Bibliography

Primary Sources: (C.R. = Corporation Records)
Manorial Survey. Inquisition Post Mortem. Cardiff City Records.
Manorial Surveys, Francis and Baker.
Original Charters of Neath, Ed. by G. Francis.
Neath Parish Records 1718-1815.
Quarter Session Records, County Record Office.
Hall Day Minute Book and County Pleas, 1806-1829 C.R.
Turnpike Trust Records, County Record Office.
Minute Books of the Neath Quarter Meetings, County Record Office.
Minutes of the Neath Borough Council Meetings, Passim Statistics supplied by the Departments of the Neath Borough Council.
Penrice and Margam Manuscripts, Vols 1-3.
Original Charters of Neath Borough Council.

Secondary Sources
Pre-History of Wales, W. F. Grimes.
The Upper Paleolithic Age in Britain, D. Garrot.
Radio-carbon dates, Oxford A.M.S. System.
(Archaeometry Datelist).
J. A. Gourlet, E. Hall, R. Hedges.
Remains of Pleistocene Man in Paviland, R. Molleson.
South Wales and the March, Wm. Rees.
The Twelve Knights of Glamorgan, R. Griffiths (Glamorgan Historian, Vol. 3).
The Roman Frontier in Wales, R. M. Wheeler.
History of Wales, Vol. I and II. J. E. Lloyd.
Original Charters of Neath and its Abbey, C. G. Francis.
Neath Abbey, Glanmor Williams ('Neath Symposium', Ed. Elis Jenkins).
The Stradlings of St Donats, Glanmor Williams (Vale of Glamorgan Series, Vol.2).
Neath Abbey Ironworks, Laurence Ince.
A History of Neath Abbey, R. Butler.
Elizabethan Wales, Dyfnallt Owen.
Dawn of the Welsh Language, K. Jackson (Wales through the Ages).
The Towns of Wales, H. Carter.
A History of Neath Abbey, W. Birch.
The Vale of Neath, D. R. Phillips.
The Lordship of Glamorgan, M. Allschul (County History, Vol.II).
Everyday Life in Wales, I. M. Davies.
The Marcher lords of Glamorgan, L. M. Pugh (County History, Vol.II).
The Manor and the Borough, S. and B. Webb.
The Parish and the County, S. and B. Webb.
In Incorporation of the Boroughs, W. Weinbottom.
Local Government in Neath, R. Till.
Copper Industry, C. Trott (Neath Symposium)

The Freedom of the Borough was conferred on the Neath R.F.C. in 1971 on the occasion of the winning of the Welsh R.U. Cup in that year when they beat Llanelli by fifteen points to nine at the Cardiff Arms Park.

Street Names, G. Taylor (Transactions of the Neath Antiquarian Society).
Jos. Tregelles Price, Personal Library.
A History of Quakers in Glamorgan, Fay Williams (M. A. Thesis).
Briton Ferry, Cliff Morgan.
A History of Social Government, Reddich and Hurst.
Charles Darwin and Alfred Russel Wallace, L. Petroneric.
A. R. Wallace, My Life, Vol.I and Vol.II.
The Quakers in Commerce, T. Empdon.
The Second Period of Quakerism, W. C. Braithwaite.